PRAISE FOR
EXCUSE ME, PROFESSOR

"In an era of economic stagnation for the vast majority of Americans, and at a time when opportunities for upward social mobility are disappearing, careful, critical thinking about economic reality and economic policy are indispensable. It is long past time to dismiss the clichés and restore economic literacy. That is why I welcome this collection of essays."
> —Robert P. George, McCormick Professor of Jurisprudence, Department of Politics, Princeton University

"An indispensable guide to confronting the socialists among us who disguise themselves as 'liberals' and 'progressives.'"
> —David Horowitz, President, David Horowitz Freedom Center

"This is just the book today's college students need to understand the world in which they live and will, soon enough, lead. I encourage every parent, grandparent, and concerned citizen who cares deeply about America's future to give copies to all of the young people they know. It may be the only time these students ever learn the truth about the way the world works."
> —Christopher Long, President, Intercollegiate Studies Institute

"Larry Reed is one of the sharpest thinkers and clearest communicators in the free-market movement. His well-organized book refutes the widespread collectivist mythology that chomps away daily at America's liberty and prosperity. Reed and his co-authors lead us through the socialists' rubble and then chart a common-sense path to good times. I learned plenty from this book, and so will you."
> —Deroy Murdock, Fox News Contributor, Senior Fellow, Atlas Network

EXCUSE ME, PROFESSOR

EXCUSE ME, PROFESSOR

CHALLENGING THE MYTHS
OF PROGRESSIVISM

LAWRENCE W. REED

EDITOR AND CO-AUTHOR

REGNERY
PUBLISHING
A Division of Salem Media Group

Regnery® is a registered trademark of Salem Communications Holding Corporation

Library of Congress Cataloging-in-Publication Data

Excuse me, professor : challenging the myths of progressivism / edited by Lawrence W. Reed ; introduction by Ron Robinson.
    pages cm
  ISBN 978-1-62157-465-1 (paperback)
  1. Free enterprise--United States. 2. Progressivism (United States politics) 3. Capitalism--Political aspects--United States. 4. United States--Politics and government--21st century. I. Reed, Lawrence W., editor of compilation.
  HB95.E968 2015
  330.973--dc23

                            2015021727

Published in the United States by
Regnery Publishing
A Division of Salem Media Group
300 New Jersey Ave NW
Washington, DC 20001
www.Regnery.com

Excuse Me, Professor is a joint project of

The Foundation for Economic Education
1718 Peachtree Street NW
Suite 1048
Atlanta, GA 30309
www.FEE.org

Young America's Foundation
11480 Commerce Park Drive
Sixth Floor
Reston, VA 20191
800-USA-1776
www.yaf.org

Manufactured in the United States of America

10 9 8 7 6 5 4 3

Books are available in quantity for promotional or premium use. For information on discounts and terms, please visit our website: www.Regnery.com.

Distributed to the trade by
Perseus Distribution
250 West 57th Street
New York, NY 10107

CONTENTS

INTRODUCTION

CLICHÉS ARE TIRED, SHOP-WORN AND OFTEN MISLEADING. SO WHY COMPILE A book of them? Because when they are deployed in the service of a flawed ideology, dressed up to appear new and refreshing, they lead well-meaning people down dead-end paths.

Though it often emanates from the ivory towers of academia, progressivism is a dead-end philosophy. Its central notion is that an educated elite should plan and engineer societies by the use of centralized power. Progressives reject many of the principles upon which America was founded, including small and limited government, individual liberty and choice, the sanctity of contract and private property, and a free market economy.

In many respects, there's little that's truly "progressive" about progressivism. One of the crucial lessons of history is that human progress happens when humans are free, yet the progressive agenda would substantially diminish freedom while promising the unachievable—a gargantuan but somehow wise and compassionate State. Because progressives can't succeed if they level with people in clear and accurate terms, they resort to an endless stream of half-truths. They've been at it for so long—more than a century—that many of those half-truths are now clichés that are widely familiar but often ineffectively answered.

Think of this collection as a handy reference guide no matter what your level of education or choice of profession may be. You don't need to be an economist or philosopher to understand what's written here. Progressive clichés are presented, then stripped of their deceptions with compelling arguments for a broad, lay audience. For people who are actively engaged in advancing liberty and combatting the fallacies of progressivism, this will be an indispensable addition to your arsenal of intellectual ammunition.

It is more than a happy coincidence that the Foundation for Economic Education (FEE) should collaborate with Young America's Foundation (YAF) in this important project. The antecedents to this book are two classic FEE publications that YAF helped distribute in the past: *Clichés of Politics*, published in 1994, and the more influential *Clichés of Socialism*, which made its first appearance in 1962. Indeed, this new collection contains a number of chapters from those two earlier works, updated for the present day. Other entries first appeared in some version in FEE's magazine, *The Freeman*. Still others are brand new, never having appeared in print anywhere.

This anthology of essays, with the exception of #52, appeared under the online series title, "Clichés of Progressivism" from April 2014 to April 2015 on the YAF and FEE websites. Our two organizations are delighted to provide this book to a large audience of both newcomers to the ideas of liberty and older friends who want updated answers to the evolving deceptions of the statist Left.

The FEE/YAF connection takes on a personal perspective with FEE's president, Lawrence W. ("Larry") Reed as the editor of this project. At the age of 14, Larry was deeply affected by the Soviet invasion of Czechoslovakia in August 1968. Within weeks, he participated in a YAF demonstration against that invasion in downtown Pittsburgh, Pennsylvania. He joined YAF and devoured the information packet provided to new members, including a subscription to *The Freeman*, Frédéric Bastiat's *The Law*, Henry Hazlitt's *Economics in One Lesson*, Henry Grady Weaver's *The Mainspring of Human Progress*, Friedrich Hayek's *The Road to Serfdom* and yes, an early edition of *Clichés of Socialism*. As Larry himself has put it, "The message was, 'If you want to be an anticommunist, you had to go deeper than just being against tanks and guns used on innocent people. You have to know economics and philosophy too, backwards and forwards.' YAF introduced me to FEE and now almost half a century later, we both are introducing our shared values to new generations of young people."

At about the same time Larry was getting his start in the "movement" for liberty, I was doing the same, working my way up from chapter founder to leadership positions within YAF. I can attest to the power of the publications and seminars FEE produced then and still does today, for they were instrumental in the evolution of my thinking too. It's been a pleasure in recent years to work with Larry to rekindle our association and thereby magnify the influence of both FEE and YAF.

Excuse Me, Professor is not meant to be the final, definitive response to a harmful ideology. Progressivism, if nothing else, has proven to be a slippery, clever beast. It's like the arcade game, "Whack a Mole." Smack one myth and another one rears its head. And the one you smacked never really vanishes; when people forget its underlying falsehood or a new generation comes along, it just reappears. This is a project that will require our attention as far into the future as the best eyes can now see.

Finally, I want to thank Rick and Jane Schwartz for inspiring and making this publication possible. Rick always seeks to have the most persuasive answer available to his employees and friends. Rick and Jane's insights help freedom's cause in so many ways.

Ron Robinson
President
Young America's Foundation
Reston, Virginia

"INCOME INEQUALITY ARISES FROM MARKET FORCES AND REQUIRES GOVERNMENT INTERVENTION"

By Max Borders

INEQUALITY IS EVERYWHERE. IN A RAINFOREST, MAHOGANY TREES TAKE UP MORE water and sunlight than all the other plants and animals. In our economic ecosystems, entrepreneurs and investors control more of the assets than the rest of us. No one worries about the mahogany trees and yet there is terrible fretting about the wealthy. In the case of ecosystems and economies, however, there are very good reasons for an unequal distribution of resources.

The sources of some forms of inequality are better than others. For example, inequality that is a consequence of crony capitalism—or what *Barron's* editor Gene Epstein refers to as "crapitalism"—is surely undesirable. Therefore, it's important for us to make a distinction between economic entrepreneurs and political entrepreneurs: the former create value for society; the latter have figured out how to transfer resources from others into their own coffers, usually by lobbying for subsidies, special favors or anti-competitive laws.

If we can ever disentangle the crapitalists from the true entrepreneurs, we can see the difference between makers and takers. And inequality that follows from honest entrepreneurship, far from indicating that something is wrong, indicates an overall flourishing. In a system where everyone is made better off through creative activity and exchange, some people are going to get wealthy. It's a natural feature of the system—a system that rewards entrepreneurs and investors for being good stewards of capital. Of course, when people are not good stewards of capital, they fail. In other words, people who make bad investments or who don't serve customers well aren't going to stay rich long.

Whenever we hear someone lamenting inequality we should immediately say "So what?" Some of the smartest (and even some of the richest) people in America confuse concerns about the poor with concerns about the assets the wealthy control. It's rooted in that old zero-sum thinking—the idea that if a poor guy doesn't have it, it's because the wealthy guy does. But one person is only better off at the expense of another under crapitalism, not under conditions of honest entrepreneurship and free exchange.

Except for those who made lots of money hiring lawyers and lobbyists instead of researchers and developers, wealthy people got rich by creating a whole lot of value for a whole lot of people. Thus, the absence of super-wealthy people would actually be a bad sign for the rest of us—especially the poor. Indeed, it would indicate one of two things: either that not much value had been created (fewer good things in our lives like iPhones and chocolate truffles) or the government had engaged in radical redistribution, removing significant incentives for people to be value creators and stewards of capital at all.

Let's face it. When resources are sitting in investments or in bank accounts, they are *not idle*. In other words, most rich people don't just stuff their millions under mattresses or take baths in gold coins. In conditions of economic stability, these resources are constantly working in the economy. In more stable conditions, a portion finds its way to a creative restaurateur in South Carolina in the form of a loan. Another portion is being used by arbitrageurs who help stabilize commodity prices. Another portion is being loaned to a nurse so she can buy her first home. Under normal circumstances, these are all good things. But when too many resources get intercepted by Uncle Sam before they get to the nodes in these economic networks, they will be squandered in the federal bureaucracy—a vortex where prosperity goes to die.

We should also remember that, due to our productive markets, most of us live like kings. Differences in assets are not the same as differences in living standards, though people tend to fetishize the former. Economist Donald Boudreaux reminds us that Bill Gates's wealth may be about 70,000 times greater than his own. But does Bill Gates ingest 70,000 times more calories than Professor Boudreaux? Are Bill Gates's meals 70,000 times tastier? Are his children educated 70,000 times better? Can he travel to Europe or to Asia 70,000 times faster or more safely? Will Gates live 70,000 times longer? Today, even the poorest segment in America live better than almost anyone in the 18th Century and better than two-thirds of the world's population.

When we hear people fretting about inequality, we should ask ourselves: Are they genuinely concerned for the poor or are they indignant about the rich? Here's how to tell the difference: Whenever someone grumbles about "the gap," ask her if she'd be willing for the rich to be even richer if it meant improved conditions for the absolute poorest among us. If she says "no" they are admitting their concern is really with what the wealthy have, not what the poor lack. If her answer is "yes," then the so-called "gap" is irrelevant. You can then go on to talk about a legitimate concern—e.g., how best to improve the conditions of the poor without paying them to be wards of the state. In other words, the meaningful conversation we should be having is about *absolute poverty*, not relative poverty.

In so many of the discussions about income inequality, there is a basic emotional dynamic at work. Someone sees they have less than another and they feel envious. Perhaps they see they have more than another and they feel guilty. Or they see that someone has more than someone else and they feel indignation. Envy, guilt, and indignation. Are these the kinds of emotions that should drive social policy? When we begin to understand that the origins of wealth—honest entrepreneurs and stewards of capital in an inherently unequal ecosystem—we can learn to leave our more primitive emotions behind.

SUMMARY

- Economic inequality, like the personality traits that make up each individual, are a defining characteristic of humanity
- When economic inequality arises naturally in the marketplace, it largely reflects the ability of individuals to serve others; when it arises from political connections, it's unfair and corrupt
- Allowing economic inequality to occur, so long as it doesn't derive from politics, inevitably raises the standard of living for society as a whole
- Concern for "the poor" is often a way to simply disguise envy or disdain for "the rich"

2

"BECAUSE WE'RE RUNNING OUT OF RESOURCES, GOVERNMENT MUST MANAGE THEM"

By Max Borders

MILTON FRIEDMAN ONCE SAID "IF YOU PUT THE FEDERAL GOVERNMENT IN CHARGE of the Sahara Desert, in five years there'd be a shortage of sand." The great economist wasn't just being cute. He's pointing to a very serious problem with government management of resources. In this chapter, we'll talk about why it's a problem. But first we should ask: Why are people so concerned that we will run out of resources? How can we find a reasonable balance between using resources and conserving them?

When most people think about resources, they think about the possibility they might be used up. And running out of resources means there will be nothing left for future generations. This scares people. So the notion goes something like: *If parents let kids get into the groceries on the first night of the camping trip, there won't be any sandwiches left for the picnic.* The parents wisely ration the resources and restrict the kids' access so that there is something left for later. People who think government should manage resources are thinking that government will behave like wise parents. But does it?

What you may not have realized is that people in the market—under certain conditions—find a balance between consumption and conservation, which one might call "sustainability." But first there has to be a complete market mechanism. This may be hard for some people to get their heads around, because most people think markets *cause* overconsumption. And certain kinds of markets can.

Healthy markets only exist under certain rules. The main rules are what we might call the Three Ps: Private property, price signals, and profit. These are the basic conditions of exchange. Without them there can be no healthy market.

Private property means that an individual has full ownership of a resource. We know who the owner is, how much they own and that right cannot be taken away arbitrarily. The owner may also have the authority to divest himself of the resource. That means we know the difference between mine and thine and in so knowing, we have one of the conditions under which to conserve, trade, or consume.

Prices are what economist Steven Horwitz calls "information wrapped in an incentive." When the price of some resource goes high enough, owners have the incentive to do any number of things. They might use less of the resource (i.e. *conserve* it), they might find new creative ways to increase the supply of the resource, or they might find a substitute, which ends up conserving the resource. Of course, we make any such choice because we expect future returns, otherwise known as *profit*. And in this equilibrium created by prices, property, and profit, markets balance use with conservation.

Consider a resource that was once highly sought after: whale blubber. Whale blubber was used as an energy resource in the 19th century. But in the case of whales, there were only two of the three Ps. Whalers had prices and profit, but no private property. The whales belonged to what is known as the Commons—which meant anyone could hunt them. Unsurprisingly they were nearly hunted to extinction. Because no one owned them, whalers had a perverse incentive to hunt them quickly. The whales rapidly became scarce. Indeed, as the number of whales went down, the price of each individual whale went up and the incentives to hunt increased. But this can't happen if there is a robust private property regime in place. If people could own whales, their incentive is not to destroy them unsustainably, but to raise them. (Ironically, fossil fuels saved the whales thanks to substitution.)

In the 19th Century American West, wild bison (buffalo) roamed the unfenced, commonly-held Plains by the millions. They were hunted nearly to extinction. By contrast, people could own and raise cattle. The use of barbed wire on private property made it feasible to do so. Today, there are far more cattle in the Plains than bison and even where bison are privately-owned, their long-term survival is now better assured than it ever was on "public" property.

Consider trees. In North America, there are more trees than there have been in over a hundred years. Not only do foresters have incentives to regrow trees they harvest, they have incentives to cut them at a sustainable rate. Of course, in certain parts of the world—like Amazonia and Africa—concerns about forest clearing are justified. What's the big difference between forests in North America and South America? In one case, forests are largely government managed and in the other they are largely privately managed.

Since 1900, U.S. forestland acreage has remained stable, unlike some regions in the world where deforestation is happening at a rapid pace. When one includes the heavily forested Northern Forests of Canada, forestland in North America since 1900 has grown by a lot, according to the UN State of the World's Forests reports.

By contrast, forests in many parts of the world are losing ground. Why are North America's forests growing while forests in other areas are being lost? Certainly the biggest factor is whether the country has the Three Ps. The absence of property rights is known as the Tragedy of the Commons. If we look at the facts around the world, places that have stable private property rights have stable forestland. Places that don't have stable property rights regimes, have tragedies of the commons— with its attendant rush to exploit. If something isn't owned, then lots of people may have incentive to use and even abuse it, and little or no incentive to take care of it or grow it bigger.

Political leaders in areas without private property rights have tried to solve the problem of over-exploitation of forestland through the application of government management—that is: simply forbid people from using the resource or have the government allocate it "sustainably." Contrary to progressive conservation clichés, neither policy works particularly well.

In the case of bans, black markets form and there is a race to exploit the resource. Poachers and illegal exploiters emerge as the problems persist. For example, black rhinos are under threat in Africa despite bans. Because the profit motive is even stronger under bans, risk takers come out of the woodwork. In the case of government allocation of resources, the process can easily be corrupted. In other words, anyone who is able to capture the regulators will be able to manipulate the process in his favor. What follows is not only corruption, but in most cases considerations of "sustainability" go by the wayside, along with all the market mechanisms that constitute the true tests of sustainability.

SUMMARY

- It is simplistic to assume that people will blindly use up what sustains them without regard to the incentive structures they face; if they have incentives to conserve, they will do so
- Private property is a powerful incentive to conserve resources. You lose if you squander what's yours
- When property is held "in common," you have a license to use and abuse resources with little incentive to nurture and improve them

3

"EQUALITY SERVES THE COMMON GOOD"

By Lawrence W. Reed

"FREE PEOPLE ARE NOT EQUAL, AND EQUAL PEOPLE ARE NOT FREE."

I wish I could remember who first said that. It ought to rank as one of the great truths of all time, and one that is fraught with profound meaning.

Equality before the law—for instance, being judged innocent or guilty based on whether or not you committed the crime, not on what color, sex, wealth class, or creed you represent—is a noble ideal and not at issue here. The "equalness" to which the statement above refers pertains to economic income or material wealth.

Put another way, then, the statement might read, "Free people will earn different incomes. Where people have the same income, they cannot be free."

Economic equality in a free society is a mirage that redistributionists envision—and too often are willing to shed both blood and treasure to accomplish. But free people are different people, so it should not come as a surprise that they earn different incomes. Our talents and abilities are not identical. We don't all work as hard. And even if we all were magically made equal in wealth tonight, we'd be unequal in the morning because some of us would spend it and some of us would save it.

To produce even a rough measure of economic equality, governments must issue the following orders and back them up with fines, penalties, or even prisons or firing squads: "Don't excel or work harder than the next guy, don't come up with any new ideas, don't take any risks, and don't do anything differently from what you did yesterday." In other words, don't be human.

The fact that free people are not equal in economic terms is not to be lamented. It is, rather, a cause for rejoicing. Economic inequality, when it derives from the voluntary interaction of creative individuals and not from political power, testifies to the fact that people are being themselves, each putting his uniqueness to work in ways that are fulfilling to himself and of value to others. As the French would say in a different context, *Vive la difference!*

People obsessed with economic equality—egalitarianism, to employ the more clinical term—do strange things. They become envious of others. They covet. They divide society into two piles: villains and victims. They spend far more time dragging someone else down than they do pulling themselves up. They're not fun to be around. And if they make it to a legislature, they can do real harm. Then they not only call the cops, they *are* the cops.

Examples of injurious laws motivated by egalitarian sentiments are, of course, legion. They form the blueprint of the modern welfare state's redistributive apparatus. A particularly classic case was the 1990 hike in excise taxes on boats, aircraft, and jewelry. The sponsors of the bill in Congress presumed that only rich people buy boats, aircraft, and jewelry. Taxing those objects would teach the rich a lesson, help narrow the gap between the proverbial "haves" and "have-nots," and raise a projected $31 million in new revenues for the federal Treasury in 1991.

What really occurred was much different. A subsequent study by economists for the Joint Economic Committee of Congress showed that the rich did not line up by the flock to be sheared: Total revenue from the new taxes in 1991 was only $16.6 million. Especially hard-hit was the boating industry, where a total of 7,600 jobs were wiped out. In the aircraft industry, 1,470 people were pink-slipped. And in jewelry manufacturing, 330 joined the jobless ranks just so congressmen could salve their egalitarian consciences.

Those lost jobs, the study revealed, prompted a $24.2 million outlay for unemployment benefits. That's right—$16.6 million came in, $24.2 million went out, for a net loss to the deficit-ridden Treasury of $7.6 million. To advance the cause of economic equality by a punitive measure, Congress succeeded in nothing more than making both itself and the rest of us a little bit poorer.

To the rabid egalitarian, however, intentions count for everything and consequences mean little. It's more important to pontificate and assail than it is to produce results that are constructive or that even live up to the stated objective. Getting Congress to undo the damage it does with bad ideas like this is always a daunting challenge.

In July 1995 economic inequality made the headlines with the publication of a study by New York University economist Edward Wolff. The latest in a long line of screeds that purport to show that free markets are making the rich richer and the poor poorer, Wolff's work was celebrated in the mainstream media. "The most telling finding," the author wrote, "is that the share of marketable net worth held by the top 1 percent, which had fallen by 10 percentage points between 1945 and 1976, rose to 39 percent in 1989, compared with 34 percent in 1983." Those at the bottom end of the income scale, meanwhile, saw their wealth erode over the period—if the Wolff study is to be believed.

On close and dispassionate inspection, however, it turns out that the study didn't tell the whole story, if indeed it told any of it. Not only did Wolff employ a very narrow measure that inherently exaggerates wealth disparity, he also ignored the mobility of individuals up and down the income scale. An editorial in the August 28, 1995, *Investor's Business Daily* laid it out straight: "Different people make up 'the wealthy' from year to year. The latest data from income-tax returns...show that most of 1979's top-earning 20 percent had fallen to a lower income bracket by 1988."

Of those who made up the bottom 20 percent in 1979, just 14.2 percent were still there in 1988. Some 20.7 percent had moved up one bracket, while 35 percent had moved up two, 25.3 percent had moved up three, and 14.7 percent had joined the top-earning 20 percent.

If economic inequality is an ailment, punishing effort and success is no cure in any event. Coercive measures that aim to redistribute wealth prompt the smart or politically well-connected "haves" to seek refuge in havens here or abroad, while the hapless "have-nots" bear the full brunt of economic decline. A more productive expenditure of time would be to work to erase the mass of intrusive government that assures that the "have-nots" are also the "can-nots."

This economic equality thing is not compassion. When it's just an idea, it's bunk. When it's public policy, it's illogic writ large.

SUMMARY

- If people are free, they will be different. That reflects their individuality and their contributions to others in the marketplace. It requires force to make them the same
- Talents, industriousness, and savings are three of many reasons why we earn different incomes in a free society
- Forcing people to be equal economically may make misguided egalitarians feel better but it does real harm to real people

4

"THE MORE COMPLEX THE SOCIETY, THE MORE GOVERNMENT CONTROL WE NEED"

By Leonard E. Read

ARGUED A COLLEGE PRESIDENT AT A RECENT SEMINAR: "YOUR FREE MARKET, private property, limited government theories were all right under the simple conditions of a century or more ago, but surely they are unworkable in today's complex economy. The more complex the society, the greater is the need for governmental control; that seems axiomatic."

It is important to expose this oft-heard, plausible, and influential fallacy because it leads directly and logically to socialistic planning. This is how a member of the seminar team answered the college president:

"Let us take the simplest possible situation—just you and I. Next, let us assume that I am as wise as any President of the United States who has held office during your lifetime. With these qualifications in mind, do you honestly think I would be competent to coercively control what you shall invent, discover, or create, what the hours of your labor shall be, what wage you shall receive, what and with whom you shall associate and exchange? Is not my incompetence demonstrably apparent in this simplest of all societies?

"Now, let us shift from the simple situation to a more complex society—to all the people in this room. What would you think of my competence to coercively control their creative actions? Or, let us contemplate a really complex situation—the 188,000,000 people of this nation (*Editor's note: now, in 2015, about 320 million*). If I were to suggest that I should take over the management of their lives and their billions of exchanges, you would think me the victim of hallucinations. Is it not obvious that the more complex an economy, the more certainly will governmental control of productive effort exert a retarding influence? Obviously, the more complex our economy, the more we should rely on the miraculous, self-adapting processes of men acting freely. No mind of man nor any combination of minds can even envision, let alone intelligently control, the countless human energy exchanges in a simple society, to say nothing of a complex one."

It is unlikely that the college president will raise that question again.

While exposing fallacies can be likened to beating out brush fires endlessly, the exercise is nonetheless self-improving as well as useful—in the sense that rear guard actions are useful. Further, one's ability to expose fallacies—a negative tactic—appears to be a necessary preface to influentially accenting the positive. Unless a person can demonstrate competence at exploding socialistic error, he is not likely to gain wide audiences for his views about the wonders wrought by men who are free.

Of all the errors heard in classrooms or elsewhere, there is not one that cannot be simply explained away. We only need to put our minds to it. The Foundation for Economic Education seeks to help those who would expose fallacies and accent the merits of freedom. The more who outdo us in rendering this kind of help, the better.

(Editor's Note: This was the first chapter in the first edition of Clichés of Socialism *when it appeared in 1962. Though the "complexity requires control" fallacy is not publicly expressed so boldly today, it is still implicit in the core assumptions of modern progressivism. Almost every new innovation gives rise to some call from some progressive somewhere to regulate it, monitor it, and sometimes even ban it. Rarely*

will a progressive reject new assignments for government, even though government has already assumed so many assignments that it manages poorly (and at a financial loss). It behooves us to point out that the more government attempts to control, the less well it will perform all of its duties, including the essential ones. Leonard Read passed away in 1983 but his wisdom as expressed here still resonates.)

SUMMARY

- Complexity does not automatically suggest centralization of power
- You and I have a full-time job managing our own respective lives; our task increases exponentially if we try to control the lives of a handful of others and it explodes beyond reason if we try to control the lives of millions

5

"INCOME INEQUALITY IS THE GREAT ECONOMIC AND MORAL CRISIS OF OUR TIME"

By Ron Robinson

AT THE HEART OF PROGRESSIVISM'S POPULARITY IS ITS IDEOLOGICALLY DRIVEN theme that income inequality is an evil in a free society.

The 20th Century's most memorable government leaders rose to power attacking income inequality in one form or another. Lenin attacked the old regime led by the czars. He overthrew its replacement government led by social democrat Alexander Kerensky because Kerensky's socialist party tolerated income inequality. Stalin followed with his persecution of the kulaks, who were the relatively more successful, mostly Ukrainian, farmers. Lenin had set the stage for Stalin's purges by labeling kulaks as "bloodsuckers, vampires, plunderers of the people and profiteers, who fatten on famine."

Hitler and his National Socialists attacked Jewish Germans for their economic success and wealth accumulation. Mao Zedong came to power promising income equality and later led the "Cultural Revolution" to enforce his vision. The Castro brothers and their secret police, the infamous Committee for the Defense of the Revolution, sought to rid Cuba of its successful entrepreneurs, lawyers, and doctors.

Essentially the same vices motivated each of these movements: envy and coveting against the successful hard-working entrepreneurial elements of their societies. Russian peasants and sailors could be taught to vilify the kulaks. Nazis found followers in the 1930s who resented the success of Jewish merchants and professionals. Mao and his Red brigades attacked anyone who wasn't in their "masses." Castro eliminated or drove away those who had their own farm, sugar, oil-distribution, or entertainment business.

The modern day progressives also rely on envy and coveting to justify raising tax rates. You can seldom find a copy of the *New York Times*, *Washington Post*, or other progressive-leaning publication that does not cite income inequality as a threat to society.

How can vices such as envy, coveting, or as the Irish would say, "begrudgery," still be such core parts of the progressive agenda in light of the results of 20th Century movements that were similarly motivated? As the late economist Milton Friedman famously noted, "A society that puts equality before freedom will get neither. A society that puts freedom before equality will get a high degree of both."

Basically, it is part of the human condition to resist conceding that someone else is more successful than you are because of different God-given talents, or because he just might be a harder worker, or because he made better decisions. The story of Cain's resentment and jealousy towards Abel, as told in various Jewish, Christian, and Muslim Scriptures, and its horrific consequences, captures how dangerous feeding off resentment can be.

Yet, it is envy, coveting, and begrudgery which are at the core of the modern day progressive belief system.

Ask modern day income redistributionists: Did you do what Kobe Bryant, Aaron Rodgers, Alexander Ovechkin, Katy Perry, Taylor Swift, or even Bill Gates or Warren Buffett did to earn their wealth? I doubt they believe so. Yet, how many Americans get tricked into dehumanizing the "wealthy" sufficiently to take comfort in slapping confiscatory taxes on them?

In fact, in American culture today, our films, television shows, academia, and the media produce more ad hominem attacks against successful business people than in all the propaganda machines of the National Socialists, Committee for the Defense of the Revolution, and Red Guards of yesteryear.

Every student knows their fellow classmates get different grades because of differing individual intelligence, attentive ability, hard work, and the level of other distractions in students' lives. So, you do not have a classroom ideological perspective that insists all grades must be equal and that "inequality" in grades must be eliminated.

You know that your efforts, or your classmates' efforts, merit different rewards. You accept that as fair. Shuffling the grades randomly, or making every grade the same, is not going to encourage scholarship and overall effort.

So, too, this is why conservatives and libertarians are not impressed by ideological claims that income inequality is worrisome, except to the extent that government interferes to choose favorites.

One of Jesus's most memorable parables dealt with three servants receiving three different sets of talents. Jesus did not suggest those talents should be re-distributed to create an equality. He was concerned with each recipient wisely using the talents he was entrusted with. If that meant the one with the most talents used his most effectively, Jesus's parable concluded with the greatest reward for him.

One final note: When progressives discuss security or foreign threats, they often ask, "If you think Al Qaeda or the Islamic State is a threat to the U.S., then why haven't you signed up to join the military?" Well, you should use this rhetorical approach when debating or discussing the "income inequality" issue with a progressive. Why don't they volunteer more of their personal income to the government than they are legally coerced to pay?

If the progressive thinks income inequality is a threat that requires action, then I ask, "Why not begin with yourself and redistribute your income? Your income is wildly unequal to the Third World poor or even the poorest Americans." Of course, the progressive is always reluctant to acknowledge that government cannot give anything to anyone without first seizing someone's wages or earnings. And the progressives seldom volunteer their own resources.

SUMMARY

- Historically, the worst demagogues demonize a group they don't like, such as "the rich," for the purposes of political gain and power lust
- Hypocritically, many progressives advocate government income redistribution in the name of "equality" but rarely run their own lives that way or spend their own money in accordance with the policies they support

6

"CAPITALISM FOSTERS GREED AND GOVERNMENT POLICY MUST TEMPER IT"

By Lawrence W. Reed

ON APRIL 19, 2014, THE COLONIAL BREAD STORE IN MY TOWN OF NEWNAN, GEORGIA, closed its doors after a decade in business. The parent company explained, "In order to focus more sharply on our core competencies, the decision was made to close some of our retail stores." A long-time patron responded in the local newspaper this way: "It's just sad. It's simply *greed* and we're on the receiving end. It's frustrating to know there isn't anything you can do about it either."

Now there's a rather expansive view of "greed" if there ever was one! Trying to make more efficient the business in which you've invested your time and money is somehow a greedy thing to do? And what is it that the disgruntled patron wishes should be done about it? Perhaps pass a law to effectively enslave the business owner and compel him to keep the store open? Who is really the greedy one here?

"Greed" is a word that flows off progressive tongues with the ease of lard on a hot griddle. It's a loaded, pejorative term that consigns whoever gets hit with it to the moral gutter. Whoever hurls it can posture self-righteously as somehow above it all, concerned only about others while the greedy wallow in evil selfishness. Thinking people should realize this is a sleazy tactic, not a thoughtful moral commentary.

Economist Thomas Sowell famously pointed out in *Barbarians Inside the Gates and Other Controversial Essays* that the "greed" accusation doesn't meet the dictionary definition of the term any more. He wrote, "I have never understood why it is 'greed' to want to keep the money you have earned but *not* greed to want to take somebody else's money."

Once upon a time, and for a very long time, "greed" meant more than just the desire for something. It meant the inordinate, obsessive worship of it that often crossed the line into actions that harmed other people. Really, *really* wanting a million bucks was not in and of itself a bad thing if you honestly worked for it, freely traded with others for it, or took risks and actually created jobs and wealth to secure it. If you worshiped the million bucks to the point of a willingness to steal for it or hire a public official to raid the Treasury on your behalf, then you were definitely a greedy person. Shame on you. If you're one of those many people today who are willing to stoop to stealing or politicking your way to wealth, you've got a lot to answer for.

"Greed" also means, to some people, an unwillingness to share what's yours with others. I suppose a father who buys a personal yacht instead of feeding his family would qualify. But that's because he is evading a personal responsibility. He owes it to the family he brought into being to properly care for them. Does the bakery owner who closes his store thereby violate some responsibility to forever serve a certain clientele? Was that ever part of some contract all parties agreed to?

Let's not forget the fundamental and critical importance of healthy self-interest in human nature. We're born with it, and thank goodness for that! I don't lament it for a second. Taking care of yourself and those you love and have responsibility for is what makes the world work. When your self-interest motivates you to do that, it means on net balance you're good for the world. You're relieving its burdens, not adding to them.

A common but misleading claim is that the Great Recession of 2008 resulted from the "greed" of the financial community. But did the desire to make money suddenly appear or intensify in the years before 2008? George Mason University economist Lawrence White pointedly explained that blaming greed for recessions doesn't get us very far. He says "It's like blaming gravity for an epidemic of plane crashes." The gravity was always there. Other factors must have interceded to create a serious anomaly. In the case of the Great Recession, those factors prominently included years of cheap money and artificially low interest rates from the Federal Reserve, acts of Congress and the bureaucracy to jawbone banks into making dubious loans for home purchases, and government entities like Fannie Mae and Freddie Mac skewing the housing market—all policies that enjoyed broad support from progressives but never from genuinely "free market" people.

The progressive perspective on "greed" is that it's a constant problem in the private sector but somehow recedes when government takes over. I wonder exactly when a politician's self-interest evaporates and his altruistic compassion kicks in? Does that happen on election night, on the day he takes office, or after he's had a chance to really get to know the folks who grease the wheels of government? When he realizes the power he has, does that make him more or less likely to want to serve himself?

The charlatan cries, "That guy over there is greedy! I will be happy to take your money to protect you from him!" Before you rush into his arms, ask some pointed questions about how the greedy suspect is doing his work and how the would-be protector proposes to do *his*.

The fact is, there's nothing about government that makes it less "greedy" than the average guy or the average institution. Indeed, there's every reason to believe that adding political power to natural self-interest is a sure-fire recipe for magnifying the harm that greed can do. Have you ever heard of corruption in government? Buying votes with promises of other people's money? Feathering one's nest by claiming "it's for the children"? Burdening generations yet unborn with the debt to pay for today's "Cowboy Poetry Festival" in Nevada (a favorite pork project of Senator Harry Reid)?

If you are an honest, self-interested person in a free market, you quickly realize that to satisfy the self-interest that some critics are quick to dismiss as "greed," you can't put a crown on your head, wrap a robe around yourself, and demand that the peasants cough up their shekels. You have to produce, create, trade, invest, employ. You have to provide goods or services that willing customers (not taxpaying captives) will choose to buy and hopefully more than just once. Your "greed" gets translated into life-enhancing things for other people. In the top-down, socialized utopia the progressives dream of, greed doesn't disappear at all. It just gets channeled into destructive directions: to satisfy it, you've got to use the political process to grab something from other people.

The "greed" charge turns out to be little more than a rhetorical device, a superficial smear intended to serve political ends. Whether or not you worship a material thing like money is largely a matter between you and your Maker, not something that can be scientifically measured and proscribed by lawmakers who are just as prone to it as you are. Don't be a sucker for it.

SUMMARY

- Greed has become a slippery term that cries out for some objective meaning; it's used these days to describe lots of behaviors that somebody doesn't like for other, sometimes hidden, reasons
- Self-interest is healthy and natural. How you put it into action in your relationships with others is what keeps it healthy or gets it off track
- Lawmakers and government are not immune to greed and, if anything, they magnify it into harmful outcomes

7

"THE FREE MARKET IGNORES THE POOR"

By Leonard E. Read

ONCE AN ACTIVITY HAS BEEN SOCIALIZED FOR A SPELL, NEARLY EVERYONE WILL concede that that's the way it should be.

Without socialized education, how would the poor get their schooling? Without the socialized post office, how would farmers receive their mail except at great expense? Without Social Security, the aged would end their years in poverty! If power and light were not socialized, consider the plight of the poor families in the Tennessee Valley!

Agreement with the idea of state absolutism follows socialization, appallingly. Why? One does not have to dig very deep for the answer.

Once an activity has been socialized, it is impossible to point out, by concrete example, how men and women in a free market could better conduct it. How, for instance, can one compare a socialized post office with private postal delivery when the latter has been outlawed? It's something like trying to explain to a people accustomed only to darkness how things would appear were there light. One can only resort to imaginative construction.

To illustrate the dilemma: During recent years, men and women in free and willing exchange (the free market) have discovered how to deliver the human voice around the earth in one twenty-seventh of a second; how to deliver an event, like a ball game, into everyone's living room, in color and in motion, at the time it is going on; how to deliver 200 people from Los Angeles to Baltimore in three hours and 19 minutes; how to deliver gas from a hole in Texas to a range in New York at low cost and without subsidy; how to deliver 64 ounces of oil from the Persian Gulf to our Eastern Seaboard—more than half-way around the earth— for less money than government will deliver a one-ounce letter across the street in one's home town. Yet, such commonplace free market phenomena as these, in the field of delivery, fail to convince most people that "the post" could be left to free market delivery without causing people to suffer.

Now, then, resort to imagination: Imagine that our federal government, at its very inception, had issued an edict to the effect that all children, from birth to adulthood, were to receive shoes and socks from the federal government "for free." Next, imagine that this practice of "free shoes and socks" had been going on for two centuries. Lastly, imagine one of our contemporaries—one with a faith in the wonders of what can be wrought when people are free—saying, "I do not believe that shoes and socks for kids should be a government responsibility. Properly, that is a responsibility of the family. This activity should never have been socialized. It is appropriately a free market activity."

What, under these circumstances, would be the response to such a stated belief? Based on what we hear on every hand, once an activity has been socialized for even a short time, the common chant would go like this, "Ah, but you would let the poor children go barefoot!"

However, in this instance, where the activity has not yet been socialized, we are able to point out that the poor children are better shod in countries where shoes and socks are a family responsibility than in countries where they are a government responsibility. We're able to demonstrate that the poor children are better shod in countries that are more free than in countries that are less free.

True, the free market ignores the poor precisely as it does not recognize the wealthy—it is "no respecter of persons." It is an organizational way of doing things featuring openness, which enables millions of people to cooperate and compete without demanding a preliminary clearance of pedigree, nationality, color, race, religion, or wealth. It demands only that each person abide by voluntary principles, that is, by fair play. The free market means willing exchange; it is impersonal justice in the economic sphere and excludes coercion, plunder, theft, protectionism, subsidies, special favors from those wielding power, and other anti-free market methods by which goods and services change hands. It opens the way for mortals to act morally because they are free to act morally.

Admittedly, human nature is defective, and its imperfections will be reflected in the market (though arguably, no more so than in government). But the free market opens the way for men to operate at their moral best, and all observation confirms that the poor fare better under these circumstances than when the way is closed, as it is under socialism.

(Editor's Note: This essay originally appeared in the first edition of Clichés of Socialism. *Barely a word has been changed and though a few numbers are dated, the essay's wisdom is as timely and relevant today as it ever was.)*

SUMMARY

- Explaining how a socialized activity could actually be done better by private, voluntary means in a free market is a little like telling a blind man what it would be like to see. But that doesn't mean we just give up and remain blind

- Examples of the wonders of free and willing exchange are all around us. We take them for granted. Just imagine what it would be like if shoes and socks had been a government monopoly for a couple hundred years, versus the variety and low cost of shoes as now provided in free countries by entrepreneurs

8

"THE ECONOMY NEEDS MORE PLANNING—*CENTRAL* PLANNING, THAT IS"

By Lawrence W. Reed

THANKSGIVING IS JUST ONE DAY EACH YEAR. BUT BECAUSE WE HAVE SO MUCH TO be thankful for, maybe it ought to be every day.

G. K. Chesterton once said, "I would maintain that thanks are the highest form of thought; and that gratitude is happiness doubled by wonder."

Think about that, especially Chesterton's use of the word "wonder." It means "awe" or "amazement." The least thankful people tend to be those who are rarely awed or amazed, in spite of the extraordinary beauty, gifts and achievements that envelop us.

A shortage of "wonder" is a source of considerable error and unhappiness in the world. What should astound us all, some take for granted or even expect as entitlements. Of those who believe more government is the answer to almost everything, some days I think they don't even notice the endless wonders that result from things *other* than the political power they worship.

We're moved by great music, sometimes to tears. We enjoy an endless stream of labor-saving, life-enriching inventions. We're surrounded by abundance in markets for everything from food to shoes to books. We travel in hours to distances that required a month of discomfort of our recent ancestors.

In America, life expectancy at age 60 is up by about eight years since 1900, while life expectancy at birth has increased by an incredible 30 years. The top three causes of death in 1900 were pneumonia, tuberculosis and diarrhea. Today, we live healthier lives and long enough to die mainly from illnesses (like heart disease and cancer) that are degenerative, aging-related problems.

Technology, communications and transportation progressed so much in the last century that hardly a library in the world could document the stunning accomplishments. I marvel that I can call a friend in China from my car or find the nearest coffee shop with an "app" on my iPhone. I'm amazed every time I take a coast-to-coast flight, while the unhappy guy next to me complains that the flight attendant doesn't have any ketchup for his omelet.

Have you ever seen a Sears catalog from 1915 and compared it to any department store catalog of today? In spite of what inflation has done to our money in the intervening century, would you rather spend a thousand dollars shopping in the 1915 catalog—with its washboards and plows—or in the catalog of today, where a thousand bucks can fetch you a wild array of electronics and labor-saving appliances?

None of these things that should inspire wonderment were inevitable, automatic or guaranteed. Almost all of them come our way by incentive, self-interest and the profit motive—from people who give their creativity to us not because they are ordered to, but because of the reward and sense of accomplishment they derive when they do. Some see this and are astonished and grateful, happy and inspired. Others see it and are envious and unappreciative, angry and demanding. Still others hardly notice, and busy themselves trying to micromanage the world according to their own grand designs.

My senses are always heightened when I'm outdoors, at least in terms of noticing nature. Plants, animals, the stars—all that "stuff" fascinates me. I want to know what this weed is called, where that bird is headed and why, and what the name of that star is. While walking my dogs recently, one natural wonder after another accosted me—fragrant honeysuckle in full bloom on a gorgeous Georgia morning, followed by a stunning spray of roses in a neighbor's yard, and upon returning to my home, the intricate, colorful clematis and braided hibiscus I planted just weeks ago. I am in constant, obsessive awe of a world so far beyond my comprehension—and so remote from *any* mortal's ability to duplicate or centrally plan.

As an economist, I'm inevitably drawn to the economic implications of these observations. No economist ever said it as well as F. A. Hayek: "The curious task of economics is to demonstrate to men how little they really know about what they imagine they can design." In his memorable Nobel Prize acceptance speech delivered in 1974, Hayek illustrated the point brilliantly: "If man is not to do more harm than good in his efforts to improve the social order, he will have to learn that…he cannot acquire the full knowledge which would make mastery of the events possible. He will therefore have to use what knowledge he can achieve, not to shape the results as the craftsman shapes his handiwork, but rather to cultivate a growth by providing the appropriate environment, in the manner in which the gardener does this for his plants."

The central planner would undoubtedly note that like a perfectly shaped bonsai tree or rose bush, some humans need a good pruning (and that very same central planner would probably be the first in line to do it, enjoying every minute of it). You can take a bonsai tree or a rose bush, cut it back or tie it up with good results. But try something comparable to your fellow citizens and you just might find they'll never leaf or bloom again.

Admittedly, the human/natural world analogy is fraught with limitations. I intend it only to provoke the reader to think, and take it as far as it holds. In the process, it will be useful to remember that humans by their very nature are not robots. We're not so easily planned for as a programmer programs a machine. When we're children, parents are our central planners but the point of adulthood is that at some point, parents should leave us alone. We tend to go further when the environment allows each of us the freedom to plan for ourselves. Amazing things happen when we do.

Leonard E. Read, FEE's founder, wrote a classic essay ("I, Pencil") in 1958 that explains an exquisite fact: No one person in the world knows how to make a simple pencil, yet pencils and far more complicated things are produced by the boatload every day. That should be a humbling thought if you think you can somehow plan an economy for millions of people.

The more one allows the world's wonders to witness to him, the less he'll want to play God with other people's lives or the economy that their trillions of individual decisions create.

One more point about "planning." The question is never whether there will *be* planning but rather, as wise observers of human society have pointed out, whether *the plans of some individuals with little power are displaced by those who have more power.* "The more the State 'plans,'" wrote Hayek, "the more difficult planning becomes for the individual."

The progressive intellectuals and their followers are in awe of what they think they might accomplish through the use of government power. They might benefit if they stopped to smell the roses. Like the rest of the natural world, what real life in a free environment *actually* accomplishes is much more awesome.

SUMMARY

- Consider the wonders all around you. Perhaps far more than you ever imagined are the result *not* of some top-down, central plan imposed by wise schemers in government but rather, of the dreams and plans of individuals and their personal initiative
- Central planning as an economic framework is rooted in what Hayek would call "a pretense to knowledge." No

group of people, no matter how much government power they possess, can possibly know more than an infinitesimal fraction of the knowledge they would have to possess to plan an economy

9

"HUMAN RIGHTS ARE MORE IMPORTANT THAN PROPERTY RIGHTS"

BY PAUL L. POIROT

―――――――――――

It is not the right of property which is protected, but the right to property. Property, per se, has no rights; but the individual—the man—has three great rights, equally sacred from arbitrary interference: the right to his life, the right to his liberty, the right to his property.... The three rights are so bound to together as to be essentially one right. To give a man his life but deny him his liberty, is to take from him all that makes his life worth living. To give him his liberty but take from him the property which is the fruit and badge of his liberty, is to still leave him a slave

—*U.S. Supreme Court Justice George Sutherland*

TRICKY PHRASES WITH FAVORABLE MEANINGS AND EMOTIONAL APPEAL ARE BEING used today to imply a distinction between *property* rights and *human* rights.

By implication, there are two sets of rights—one belonging to human beings and the other to property. Since human beings are more important, it is natural for the unwary to react in favor of *human* rights.

Actually, there is no such distinction between property rights and human rights. The term *property* has no significance except as it applies to something owned by someone. Property itself has neither rights nor value, except as human interests are involved. There are no rights but human rights, and what are spoken of as property rights are only the human rights of individuals to property.

What are the property rights thus disparaged by being set apart from human rights? They are among the most ancient and basic of human rights, and among the most essential to freedom and progress. They are the privileges of private ownership which give meaning to the right to the product of one's labor—privileges which men have always regarded instinctively as belonging to them almost as intimately and inseparably as their own bodies. Unless people can feel secure in their ability to retain the fruits of their labor, there is little incentive to save and expand the fund of capital—the tools and equipment for production and for better living.

The Bill of Rights in the United States Constitution recognizes no distinction between property rights and other human rights. The ban against unreasonable search and seizure covers "persons, houses, papers, and effects," without discrimination. No person may, without due process of law, be deprived of "life, liberty or property"; all are equally inviolable. The right to trial by jury is assured in criminal and civil cases alike. Excessive bail, excessive fines, and cruel and unusual punishments are grouped in a single prohibition. The Founding Fathers realized that a man or woman without property rights—without the right to the product of his own labor—is not a free man.

These constitutional rights all have two characteristics in common. First, they apply equally to all persons. Second, they are, without exception, guarantees of freedom or immunity from governmental interference. They are not assertions of claims against others, individually or collectively. They merely say, in effect, that there are certain human liberties, including some pertaining to property, which are essential to free citizens and upon which the state shall not infringe.

Now what about the so-called human rights that are represented as superior to property rights? What about the "right" to a job, the "right" to a standard of living, the "right" to a minimum wage or a maximum work week, the right to a "fair" price, the "right" to bargain collectively, the "right" to security against the adversities and hazards of life, such as old age and disability?

The framers of the Constitution would have been astonished to hear these things spoken of as rights. They are not immunities from governmental compulsion; on the contrary, they are demands for new forms of governmental compulsion. They are not claims to the product of one's own labor; they are, in some if not in most cases, claims to the products of other people's labor.

These "human rights" are indeed different from property rights, for they rest on a denial of the basic concept of property rights. They are not freedoms or immunities assured to all persons alike. They are special privileges conferred upon some persons at the expense of others. The real distinction is not between property rights and human rights, but between equality of protection from governmental compulsion on the one hand and demands for the exercise of such compulsion for the benefit of favored groups on the other.

(Editor's Note: This essay was first published in 1962.)

SUMMARY

- You own yourself and you own those material things you've created or traded for freely with others. These are rights to property—property in yourself and in your possessions— and cannot be separated from human rights
- America's Founders made no distinction between "human rights" and "property rights" for good reason: there aren't any. They are one and the same
- Your right to what's yours is very different from a claim on the person or property of others

10

"I HAVE A RIGHT!"

BY CHARLES W. BAIRD

LOTS OF PEOPLE MAKE THIS CLAIM WITHOUT EVEN THINKING ABOUT THE NATURE and source of rights. What are rights, and where do they come from?

The progressive or interventionist view is that so long as legislation is adopted under the rules of procedural due process, government creates and extinguishes rights. For example, Congress, by following the rules of legislative process outlined in the Constitution, can create or extinguish a right to a job, a right to an education, or a right to food.

When progressives wish to expand the scope of government they often make a distinction between a "privilege" and a "right." In this view, something is a privilege only if a person can acquire it through his own means; and something is a right if government uses tax money or other coercive powers to provide it to individuals irrespective of their means. Really important things, they say, ought to be rights, not privileges. Thus health care in America was once a privilege, but now it's touted in both rhetoric and law as a right.

In the Declaration of Independence, Thomas Jefferson wrote about "unalienable" rights that all individuals have irrespective of government. According to him, all humans are "endowed" with these rights by God. Some of Jefferson's colleagues said that "nature" endowed humans with rights—i.e., that rights are inherent in human nature. In either case, rights are logically prior to government. Government has no legitimate authority to add to or subtract from such rights. Its role is to protect them.

If something is a human right in the Jeffersonian sense, it applies to all individuals merely by virtue of their humanity. If one person has such a right, all other humans must logically have the same right. One cannot, without self-contradiction, claim a human right for himself and deny it to others. To do so would be to admit that the right is not a "human" right.

Moreover, it must be possible for all individuals to exercise the claimed right simultaneously without logical contradiction. If when I exercise a right I have claimed, it is thereby impossible for someone else to exercise the identical right at the same time, my action implies that the alleged right does not inhere in human nature. My action implies that it is my right and not the right of the other person.

For example, suppose I claim a right to a job. If that claim means that I will be employed any time I wish to be (what else could it mean?), there must be some other person who has the duty to provide the job. But then that other person does not have the same right I have. My right is to be employed, his "right" is to provide the job. My right creates a *duty* for him to undertake some positive action that he may not want to undertake. Notwithstanding that we both are human, his freedom of choice is subordinated to my freedom of choice.

Is there any job-related fundamental human right in the Jeffersonian sense? Yes, it is the right of all individuals to offer to buy or sell labor services at any terms they choose. I have a right to offer to sell my labor services at terms I like, and so do you. We all can exercise that right without thereby denying it to anyone else. I have a right to offer to buy (employ) the labor services of any other person at terms I like, and so do you. We can do so without thereby denying the right to anyone else. Those to whom you and I extend our offers are free to reject them. In exercising these rights we impose no duty to undertake any positive action on any other person.

Apply the same test to the right to food, the right to an education, and the right to health care. Are any of these fundamental human rights? If they are interpreted to mean that individuals will receive food, education, and health care no matter what other people want, they are not fundamental human rights. We all have a fundamental right to *offer* to buy or sell food, education services, and health care at any terms we like, but if we cannot find others who are willing to accept our offers, we have no right to force them to do so.

Apply the same test to the rights guaranteed by the First Amendment: freedom of religion, freedom of association, freedom of speech, and freedom of the press. These are all fundamental human rights. We each can exercise free choice of religion without denying that right to others. Note, however, we have no right to join a religious organization that doesn't want to accept us. We each can associate with any individuals or groups, but only so long as they are willing to associate with us. Exercising that right does not make it impossible for others to do the same. We each can say what we like without denying that same right to others. Note again, however, we have no right to force people to listen, or to provide us with a forum in which to speak. We each are free to try to assemble the necessary resources, by voluntary agreements with others, to publish a newspaper or a magazine (or a blog). But we have no right to force people to provide those necessary resources or to purchase or read our publications.

Note that the progressive and the Jeffersonian views of rights are not only different, they are incompatible. Any time a right claimed by anyone imposes a duty on another to undertake positive action, the alleged right cannot possibly be exercised by both simultaneously without logical contradiction.

The progressive view of rights is often called the positivist view because such rights necessarily impose duties to undertake positive actions on others. It is part of a larger philosophy called legal positivism which asserts that rights are whatever government says they are.

The Jeffersonian view of rights is often called the negative view because the only duty imposed on others by such rights is a duty to *refrain* from undertaking a particular action. It is a duty to refrain from interfering with others. Moreover, in this view, government itself is bound by the rights justly claimed by all individuals.

The next time you say, "I have a right," ask: "Who has the duty?" If there is anyone who has a duty to do anything except refrain from interfering with you, ask: "On what grounds do I claim a right to subordinate that person's will to mine?"

(Editor's Note: This essay appeared as the first chapter in FEE's 1994 anthology, Clichés of Politics.*)*

SUMMARY

- Genuine rights are prior to government; they are part of your nature as an individual human
- The desire to have something doesn't automatically mean you have a right to it
- If your alleged "right" to something cannot be achieved without forcing another person to provide it for you, then it wasn't a "right" to begin with
- You have a right to read a book but no right to compel someone else to give you one

11

"RICH PEOPLE HAVE AN OBLIGATION TO GIVE BACK"

By Lawrence W. Reed

FOR A SOCIETY THAT HAS FED, CLOTHED, HOUSED, CARED FOR, INFORMED, ENTERTAINED, and otherwise enriched more people at higher levels than any in the history of the planet, there sure is a lot of groundless guilt in America.

Manifestations of that guilt abound. The example that peeves me the most is the one we often hear from well-meaning philanthropists who adorn their charitable giving with this little chestnut: "I want to give something back." It always sounds as though they're apologizing for having been successful.

Translated, that statement means something like this: "I've accumulated some wealth over the years. Never mind how I did it, I just feel guilty for having done it. There's something wrong with my having more than somebody else, but don't ask me to explain how or why because it's just a fuzzy, uneasy feeling on my part. Because I have something, I feel obligated to have less of it. It makes me feel good to give it away because doing so expunges me of the sin of having it in the first place. Now I'm a good guy, am I not?"

It was apparent to me how deeply ingrained this mindset has become when I visited the gravesite of John D. Rockefeller at Lakeview Cemetery in Cleveland a few years ago. The wording on a nearby plaque commemorating the life of this remarkable entrepreneur implied that giving much of his fortune away was as worthy an achievement as building the great international enterprise, Standard Oil, that produced it in the first place. The history books most kids learn from these days go a step further. They routinely criticize people like Rockefeller for the wealth they created and for the profit motive, or self-interest, that played a part in their creating it, while lauding them for relieving themselves of the money.

More than once, philanthropists have bestowed contributions on my organization and explained they were "giving something back." They meant that by giving to us, they were paying some debt to society at large. It turns out that, with few exceptions, these philanthropists really had not done anything wrong.

They made money in their lives, to be sure, but they didn't steal it. They took risks they didn't have to. They invested their own funds, or what they first borrowed and later paid back with interest. They created jobs, paid market wages to willing workers, and thereby generated livelihoods for thousands of families. They invented things that didn't exist before, some of which saved lives and made us healthier. They manufactured products and provided services, for which they asked and received market prices.

They had willing and eager customers who came back for more again and again. They had stockholders to whom they had to offer favorable returns. They also had competitors, and had to stay on top of things or lose out to them. They didn't use force to get where they got; they relied on free exchange and voluntary contract. They paid their bills and debts in full. And every year they donated some of their profits to lots of community charities no law required them to support. Not a one of them that I know ever did any jail time for anything.

So how is it that anybody can add all that up and still feel guilty? I suspect that if they are genuinely guilty of anything, it's allowing themselves to be intimidated by the losers and the envious of the world—the people who are in the redistribution business either because they don't know how to create anything or they simply choose the easy way out. They just take what they want, or hire politicians to take it for them.

Or like a few in the clergy who think that wealth is not made but simply "collected," the redistributionists lay a guilt trip on people until they disgorge their lucre—notwithstanding the Tenth Commandment against coveting. Certainly, people of faith have an obligation to support their church, mosque, or synagogue, but that's another matter and not at issue here.

A person who breaches a contract owes something, but it's to the specific party on the other side of the deal. Steal someone else's property and you owe it to the person you stole it from, not society, to give it back. Those obligations are real and they stem from a voluntary agreement in the first instance or from an immoral act of theft in the second. This business of "giving something back" simply because you earned it amounts to manufacturing mystical obligations where none exist in reality. It turns the whole concept of "debt" on its head. To give it "back" means it wasn't yours in the first place, but the creation of wealth through private initiative and voluntary exchange does not involve the expropriation of anyone's rightful property.

How can it possibly be otherwise? By what rational measure does a successful person in a free market, who has made good on all his debts and obligations in the traditional sense, owe something further to a nebulous entity called society? If Entrepreneur X earns a billion dollars and Entrepreneur Y earns two billion, would it make sense to say that Y should "give back" twice as much as X? And if so, who should decide to whom he owes it? Clearly, the whole notion of "giving something back" just because you have it is built on intellectual quicksand.

Successful people who earn their wealth through free and peaceful exchange may choose to give some of it away, but they'd be no less moral and no less debt-free if they gave away nothing. It cheapens the powerful

charitable impulse that all but a few people possess to suggest that charity is equivalent to debt service or that it should be motivated by any
degree of guilt or self-flagellation.

A partial list of those who honestly do have an obligation to give
something back would include bank robbers, shoplifters, scam artists,
deadbeats, and politicians who "bring home the bacon." They have good
reason to feel guilt, because they're guilty.

But if you are an exemplar of the free and entrepreneurial society,
one who has truly earned and husbanded what you have and have done
nothing to injure the lives, property, or rights of others, you are a different breed altogether. When you give, you should do so because of the
personal satisfaction you derive from supporting worthy causes, not
because you need to salve a guilty conscience.

*(Editor's Note: Versions of this essay have previously appeared in
FEE's magazine,* The Freeman, *under the title,* "Who Owes What To
Whom?")

SUMMARY

- The innocent-sounding phrase, "I want to give back," far
  too often implies guilt for having been productive or successful
- If you earned it through wealth-creation followed by free
  and voluntary exchange, don't let others get away with making you feel guilty just because you have it
- The people who really should "give it back" are those to
  whom it doesn't belong, or who took it from others in the
  first place

12

"I PREFER SECURITY TO FREEDOM"

By Leonard E. Read

MANY PEOPLE WANDER UNWITTINGLY INTO SOCIALISM, GULLED BY ASSUMPTIONS they have not tested. One popular but misleading assumption is that security and freedom are mutually exclusive alternatives—that to choose one is to forego the other.

In the United States during the past century, more people achieved greater material security than their ancestors had ever known in any previous society. Large numbers of people in this country accumulated a comfortable nest egg, so that "come hell or high water"—depressions, old age, sickness or whatever—they could rely on the saved fruits of their own labor (and/or that of family members, friends or parishioners) to carry them through any storm or temporary setback. By reason of unprecedented freedom of choice, unparalleled opportunities, provident living, and the right to the fruits of their own labor—private property— they were able to meet the many exigencies which arise in the course of a lifetime.

We think of these enviable, personal achievements as *security*. But this type of security is not an alternative to freedom; rather, it is an outgrowth of freedom. This traditional security stems from freedom as the oak from an acorn. It is not a case of either/or; one without the other is impossible. Freedom sets the stage for all the security available in this uncertain world.

Security in its traditional sense, however, is not what the progressives are talking about when they ask, "Wouldn't you rather have security than freedom?" They have in mind what Maxwell Anderson called "the guaranteed life," or the arrangement described by Karl Marx, "from each according to his ability, to each according to his need." Under this dispensation, the political apparatus, having nothing at its disposal except the police force, uses this force to take the property of the more well-to-do in order to dispense the loot among the less well-to-do. In theory, at least, that's all there is to it—a leveling procedure!

Admittedly, this procedure appears to attract millions of our fellow citizens. It relieves them, they assume, of the necessity of looking after themselves; Uncle Sam is standing by with bags of forcibly collected largess.

To the unwary, this looks like a choice between security and freedom. But, in fact, it is the choice between the self-responsibility of a free man or the slave-like security of a ward of the government. Thus, if a person were to say, "I prefer being a ward of the government to exercising the personal practice of freedom," he would at least be stating the alternatives in correct terms.

One need not be a profound sociologist to realize that the ward-of-the-government type of "security" does preclude freedom for all three parties involved. Those from whom property is taken obviously are denied the freedom to use what they've earned from their labor. Secondly, people to whom the property is given—who get something for nothing—are forfeiting the most important reason for living: the freedom to be responsible for self. The third party in this setup—the authoritarian who does the taking and the giving—also loses his freedom.

One need not be a skilled economist to understand how the guaranteed life leads to general insecurity. Whenever government assumes responsibility for the security, welfare, and prosperity of citizens, the costs of government rise beyond the point where it is politically expedient to cover them by direct tax levies. At this point—usually 20-25 percent of the people's earned income—the government resorts to deficit financing and inflation. Inflation—increasing the volume of the money supply to cover deficits—means a dilution of the money's purchasing power. Unless arrested by a change in thinking and in policy, this process leads to all "guarantees" becoming worthless, and a general insecurity follows.

The true and realistic alternatives are *insecurity* or *security*. Insecurity must follow the transfer of responsibility from self to others, particularly when transferred to arbitrary and capricious government. Genuine security is a matter of self-responsibility, based on the right to the fruits of one's own labor and the freedom to trade.

(Editor's Note: This essay, minus some slight edits for updating, was originally published in 1962 in FEE's book, Clichés of Socialism.*)*

SUMMARY

- True security is an outgrowth of freedom, not an alternative to it
- Being dependent, instead of being independent, is a move away from true security
- Mr. Read's observation more than half a century ago that increasing reliance on a welfare state for security would produce financial problems seems positively prescient today. Consider our $17.5 trillion national debt as evidence
- The real choice is not between freedom and security but between security and insecurity

13

"COOPERATION, NOT COMPETITION!"

BY LAWRENCE W. REED

"GYM NOW STRESSES COOPERATION, NOT COMPETITION," BLARED A HEADLINE IN the *New York Times* a decade ago. The story was about an elementary school where "confrontational" games, team sports, and elimination rounds were changed or scrapped so that differences between students' athletic abilities would be minimized.

Perhaps this is fine for grade-school gym class, but it would make for rather boring Olympic Games. Were it imposed on production and trade, it would condemn millions to poverty and early death. Let's review some fundamental principles.

In economics, competition is not the antithesis of cooperation; rather, it is one of its highest and most beneficial forms. That may seem counterintuitive. Doesn't competition necessitate rivalrous or even "dog-eat-dog" behavior? Don't some competitors lose?

In my view, competition in the marketplace means nothing less than striving for excellence in the service of others for self-benefit. In other words, sellers cooperate with consumers by catering to their needs and preferences.

Many people think that competition is directly related to the number of sellers in a market: The more sellers there are, or the smaller the share of the market any one of them has, the more competitive the market. But competition can be just as fierce between two or three rivals as it can be among 10 or 20.

Moreover, market share is a slippery notion. Almost any market can be defined narrowly enough to make someone look like a monopolist instead of a competitor. I have a 100 percent share of the market for articles by Lawrence Reed, for example. I have a far smaller share of the market for articles generally.

Not so long ago, XM and Sirius were the only two satellite-radio providers in the United States. For a year and a half the federal government prevented the two from merging, fearing that a harmful monopoly would result. Economists argued that XM and Sirius were competing not only with each other but as two of many companies in a huge media marketplace that includes free radio, iPods and other MP3 players, Internet radio stations, cable radio services, and even cell phones—all of which, along with likely new technologies, would continue to compete even after the merger. Ultimately, economic reasoning prevailed and the merger was allowed.

Governments don't have to decree competition; all they have to do is prevent and punish force, violence, deception, and breach of contract. Enterprising individuals will compete because it is in their financial interest to do so, even if they'd prefer not to.

Competition spurs creativity and innovation and encourages producers to cut costs. You wouldn't think of stopping the Kentucky Derby in the middle of the race and complain that one of the horses was ahead. The same should be true of free markets, where the race never ends and competitors enter and leave continuously.

Theoretically, there are two kinds of monopoly: coercive and efficiency. A coercive monopoly results from a government grant of exclusive privilege. Government, in effect, must take sides in the market to give birth to a coercive monopoly. It must make it difficult, costly, or impossible for anyone but the favored firm to do business. The U.S. Postal Service is an example. By law no one else can deliver first-class mail.

In other cases the government may not ban competition outright but simply bestow privileges, immunities, or subsidies on one or more firms while imposing costly requirements on all others. Regardless of the method, a firm that enjoys a coercive monopoly is in a position to harm consumers and get away with it.

An efficiency monopoly, by contrast, earns a high share of a market because it does the best job. It receives no special favors from the law. Others are free to compete and, if consumers so will it, to grow as big as the "monopoly." Indeed, an efficiency monopoly is not much of a monopoly at all in the traditional sense. It doesn't restrict output, raise prices, and stifle innovation; it actually sells more and more by pleasing customers and attracting new ones while improving both product and service.

An efficiency monopoly has no legal power to compel people to deal with it or to protect itself from the consequences of its unethical practices. An efficiency monopoly that turns its back on the very performance which produced its success would be, in effect, posting a sign that reads, "COMPETITORS WANTED."

Where does antitrust law come into all this? From its very inception in 1890, antitrust has been plagued by vagaries, false premises, and a stagnant conception of dynamic markets.

The Sherman Antitrust Act of 1890 put the government on record as officially favoring competition and opposing monopoly without ever coming close to any solid definition of either term. It simply made it a criminal offense to "monopolize" or "attempt to monopolize" a market without ever saying what kind of actions qualified.

The first lawsuit the government filed ended disastrously for the Justice Department: The Supreme Court ruled in 1895 that the American Sugar Refining Company was not guilty of becoming a monopolist when it merged with the E. C. Knight Company. The evidence suggested that the merged companies would have made for a very strange monopoly indeed—one that substantially increased output and greatly cut prices to consumers.

In *The Antitrust Religion* (Cato, 2007), Edwin S. Rockefeller explains how the self-serving legal community invented sinister-sounding terms for quite natural phenomena and at the same time enjoys a feeling of self-righteousness in "protecting" the public from those evils. Such terms include "reciprocity" ("I won't buy from you unless you buy from me"); "exclusive dealing" ("I won't sell to you if you buy from anyone else"); and "bundling" ("Even though you only want Chapter One, you have to buy the whole book.") Another work I strongly recommend on this subject is a classic by economist D. T. Armentano, *The Myths of Antitrust*.

In a free market unencumbered by anticompetitive intrusions from government, these factors ensure that no firm in the long run, regardless of size, can charge and get any price it wants:

1. Free entry of newcomers to the field, whether they be two guys in their garage or a giant firm that sees an opportunity to expand into a new product line.
2. Foreign competition. As long as government doesn't hamper international trade, this is always a potent force.
3. Competition of substitutes. People are often able to substitute a product different from yet similar to the monopolist's.
4. Competition of all goods for the consumer's dollar. Every business competes with every other business for consumers' limited dollars.
5. Elasticity of demand. At higher prices, some people will buy less.

Bottom line: Consider competition in a free market not as a static phenomenon but rather as a dynamic, never-ending leapfrog process in which the leader today can be the follower tomorrow.

SUMMARY

- Competition is actually a very important kind of cooperation: It prompts people to serve others in the best ways they know how
- A company that gets a high market share because of its efficiency and service is both competitive and cooperative in the sense that it earns the satisfaction and patronage of customers
- An economy without competition would be larded with waste and indifference
- The core assumptions of antitrust law are dubious and nebulous

14

"HEALTHCARE IS A RIGHT"

By Max Borders

HEALTHCARE IS IMPORTANT. PEOPLE GET SICK AND INJURED. AS COMPASSIONATE human beings, we should do what we can, within reason, to see that people are treated—especially when they don't have the means to get treatment themselves. We can build and support charity hospitals. We can volunteer for free clinics. We can take sensible policy measures that will reduce the costs and increase the access to medical goods and services.

But we cannot pretend that healthcare is a right.

This sort of verbiage is just that—verbiage, until it requires enforcement. And if you have been tempted to think of basic needs as being rights, remember this: Rights confer duties upon others. That has tremendous implications for any healthcare system.

Think about a right of free speech. That right confers a duty onto others not to interfere with or mute your expression, as long as you're not harming or threatening anyone. But when it comes to certain other purported rights involving things that must be *produced by others*, like education or healthcare, that means others have a duty to produce that good or service. Once we slide from the apparently benevolent talk of people having rights, to the reality that other people will then have enforced duties to produce that right, we also slide from individual compassion to state compulsion. In other words, any such right necessarily conflicts with others' rights not to be treated as means to some end.

In the process of outsourcing our sense of compassion to a central producer of healthcare goods and services, we cede our healthcare choices—and charitable instincts—to a central authority. How else is the government going to ensure that healthcare is produced, by right, for everyone?

This central authority, with its attendant healthcare bureaucracy, is not very good at figuring out who needs what and how much they need of it. Socialized, or "single payer" healthcare systems that are meant to allocate healthcare goods and services have very different incentives than systems in which people exchange goods and services freely.

In the Soviet Union, planners had no price system to help them determine how many shoes were needed in Minsk or boots were needed in Moscow. Supply and demand was guesswork and "targets"—with all the attendant problems of political allocation, buck passing and waiting lines. The Soviet economy, marked by shortages and gluts, could not very effectively be planned. The same can be said about the modern single-payer healthcare system.

Consider our neighbors in Canada. In the Fraser Institute's annual report, "Waiting Your Turn: Wait Times for Health Care in Canada," the Canadian think tank says the median wait time in 2013 hit 18.2 weeks, three days longer than in 2012. The average wait time for ortho-pedic surgery, in particular, reached 39.6 weeks for treatment, while patients waited an average 17.4 weeks for an appointment with a neuro-surgeon. During this time, people were suffering. Some even died. Yet all of this is happening in a country where healthcare is considered a right that confers duties on taxpayers. Can the suffering that flows from rationing be considered compassionate? If treating healthcare as a right has these sorts of perverse consequences, shouldn't that lead us to question all such rights talk?

Put another way: Let's grant for a moment that healthcare is a right, or, at least, let's assume everyone wants healthcare to be something that our fellow citizens have access to. If we all agreed to that, what if we determined that a free market in medical care allowed more people to gain greater access to healthcare goods and services in a timely manner? Would a "right" to healthcare then confer duties upon policymakers to introduce measures that would make the healthcare market freer, for example:

- Let people choose less expensive health insurance policies and policy options that fit their circumstances and budgets—across state lines and free of some or all of the state mandates that price low-income people out of the marketplace?
- Encourage policies that restore a functioning price system to healthcare so that people can make wiser purchasing decisions, all of which will help rein in spiraling costs?
- Allow individuals, not just employers, to get a tax deduction when they buy health insurance, which would make insurance more personal and portable?
- Dismantle any and all healthcare schemes (like Medicare) that provide subsidies for the rich and tax the poor and middle class in the process?
- Remove barriers to competition such as professional licensing, certificates of need, and other regulations that hike costs and limit access?
- Encourage people to use financial healthcare products like Health Savings Accounts, which give people incentives a) to be wise healthcare consumers, and b) to save resources for future healthcare needs and c) to invest in preventive measures?

Combined, the measures listed above would revolutionize the healthcare system in terms of price, quality, innovation, and access by the least advantaged. Talk of "rights" is just a rhetorical game progressives play to get the policies they want (usually a single payer system). But talk of "rights" does nothing for the goal of actually figuring out how to get people reasonable access to the healthcare they need. To do that, we have to deal directly with the problems of affordability (as in the U.S.) or with the perverse consequences of rationing (as in Canada). The disastrous rollout of Obamacare just might stimulate a serious, widespread discussion of these options for the first time.

Yes, healthcare is something we'll all need at one time or another. But it is not a right. If we really care about people getting healthcare, let's focus on how to reform the system for good—so that free people can generate abundance in healthcare. If we can do it for mobile devices, we can do it for medicine.

SUMMARY

- Claiming that one has a right to healthcare is rhetorical exercise. The rubber hits the road when it's actually enforced, which means somebody has to be compelled to provide it or pay for it
- Centralizing healthcare decisions is a movement in the wrong direction, away from the individual consumer and toward planners who have no special knowledge that would allow them to make good decisions for others
- Market-based, consumer-focused options for healthcare deserve more serious consideration

15

"WE ARE DESTROYING THE EARTH AND GOVERNMENT MUST DO SOMETHING"

By Sandy Ikeda

PEOPLE OFTEN COMPLAIN THAT MANKIND IS DESTROYING THE EARTH: THAT INSATIABLE consumption and relentless production have laid waste to irreplaceable swaths of our planet, and that these activities have to stop or someday it will all be gone. Which raises the question: What does it means to "destroy" something?

When you burn a log, the log is destroyed but heat, light, smoke, and ashes remain. It's in that sense that physics tells us that matter is neither created nor destroyed. Similarly, cutting down a forest destroys the forest but in its place are houses and furniture and suburbs.

The real question is: Is it worth it?

What people usually mean when they say mankind is destroying the earth is that human action causes a change they don't like. It sounds odd to say that my wife, by eating a piece of toast for breakfast, is "destroying" the toast. But if I wanted that toast for myself, I might well regard her action as destructive. Same action, but the interpretation depends on purpose and context.

When a missile obliterates a building and kills the people in it, it may serve a political purpose even though the friends and family of those killed and the owners of the building are harmed. The perpetrator's gain is the victim's loss. In the political realm, one person's gain is necessarily another person's loss. You rob Peter to pay Paul; you kill Jack to appease Jill. It's a "zero-sum game."

In the economic realm, however, a thing is destroyed to the extent that it loses its usefulness to somebody for doing something. Someone may want to bulldoze my lovely home just for fun. If she pays me enough I may let her do it and be glad she did. When not physically coerced, a trade won't happen unless each side expects to gain. If it does happen, and if the people who traded are right, then all do in fact gain. Each is better off than before. The trade has created something–value. If they are wrong, they destroy value and suffer a loss, which gives them an incentive to avoid making mistakes.

In free markets, gains manifest themselves in profit, either monetary or psychic. (In the short run, of course, you can sustain a monetary loss if you think there's a worthwhile non-monetary aspect to the trade that will preserve the profit.) Now, the free market is not perfect, despite what some economics professors say about the benefits of so-called "perfect competition." People don't have complete or perfect knowledge and so they make mistakes. They trade when they shouldn't, or they don't trade when they should. Fortunately, profits and losses serve as feedback to guide their decisions.

There's another source of market imperfection. People may be capable of making good decisions but they don't trade, or trade too much, because the property rights to the things they would like to trade aren't well-defined or aren't effectively enforced. In such cases their actions or inactions create costs they don't bear or benefits they don't receive. The result is that their decisions end up destroying value.

If I free-ride off the oceans, if for example I don't pay for dumping garbage into it, then the oceans will become more polluted than they should be. If there is a cleaner, more efficient source of energy than fossil fuels, but no one can profitably use it because the state prevents anyone from doing so (for example by prohibitions or excessive taxation), then again the value that would have been created will never appear.

Our esthetic sense of beauty is part of what makes us human. If we wish to protect a lake or a valley from development because we think it beautiful, how do we do that?

To some extent it's possible to do what the Nature Conservancy does, and purchase the land that we want to protect. But that's not always possible, especially when the land is controlled not by private persons but by the state, which makes special deals with crony capitalists in so-called public-private developments. In any case, even the free market is not perfect. Economic development and material well-being mean that some beautiful landscapes and irreplaceable resources will be changed in ways not everyone will approve.

Remember, though, that economics teaches us that *an action is always taken by someone for something*. There are no disembodied costs, benefits, and values. In a world of scarcity, John believes saving rain forests is more important than saving the whales. Mary believes the opposite. If we are to get past disagreements on esthetics—essentially differences of opinion—that can turn into violent conflict, we need to find some way to settle our differences peacefully, some way to transform them into value-creating interactions.

Imperfect though it may be, the free market has so far been the most effective method we know of for doing that.

SUMMARY

- Physics teaches us that matter is not really destroyed but rather, *transformed*, so the ever-present question is, "Is it *worth* it?"
- Market transactions transform resources, as well as ownership of them, and if enhanced value doesn't result from those transactions, the resulting losses tend to minimize future mistakes

16

"OWNERSHIP MUST BE TEMPERED BY SHARING"

BY LAWRENCE W. REED

PROGRESSIVES HAVE A PROBLEM WITH OWNERSHIP, ESPECIALLY WHEN IT'S YOURS.
The very notion seems to conjure up in their minds an anti-social acquisitiveness, selfishness and greed. Far more quickly, they come to the defense of "sharing" because it suggests sacrificing ownership for the sake of others. Indeed, the most regressive Progressive is drawn to the idea of *common* ownership, in which no one in particular owns anything and somehow we all will own everything and share it equally.

The progressives' hostility to ownership is neither well-founded nor consistent. While they have a visceral distaste for private ownership (and busy themselves taxing, regulating, seizing and redistributing it), they have few problems with state ownership. It's as if men are devilish with what's theirs but angelic when it's somebody else's. This is not a concept that explains life on any planet of which I am personally aware.

The fact is, "ownership" as a *general* concept is never really at issue in any society. It is neither possible nor desirable to construct a society in which people or the material things they create are not "owned." Either you will own yourself or someone else will own you. As far as material things are concerned, somebody must own them too. Those "somebodies" will either be those who created them, received them as a gift, or traded freely for them, or they will be those who take them by force. There is no middle ground, no "third way" in which ownership is somehow avoided.

Indeed, ownership is both a virtue and a necessity. What is yours, you tend to husband. If it belongs to someone else, you have little incentive to care for it. If it belongs to "everyone"—the nebulous, collectivist approach—then you have every incentive to use and abuse it. That's why over thousands of years of historical experience, life continually reinforces this essential axiom: *the more the government owns and thereby controls, the less free and productive the people are.*

Ownership is nothing less than the right to shape, use, and dispose. Even if you have legal title to something, you wouldn't think you really owned it if the government told you what you could do with it, how, and when; in that instance, the government would be the de facto owner. In a real sense, ownership is control and the actual owner of anything is the controller.

For thoroughly trashing the resources of any society, no more sure-fire prescription exists than to take them from those to whom they belong (the rightful owners) and give them to those who are convinced in the fantasyland of their own minds that they have a better idea of what to do with them. Think "Soviet." Socialist regimes, which take from some and give to others at the point of a gun, have their cockamamie schemes for how to squander the loot, but they display an infantile ignorance of how to create wealth in the first place.

Much has been made in the past about alleged differences between fascism and communism. Sure, the Nazis invaded Stalinist Russia (after the two had made a deal to squash and divide Poland), but that was a dispute between thieves that proved the old adage that there's no honor among them. On the question of ownership, the difference was a cosmetic one that ultimately mattered little to the ordinary citizen.

Communists didn't let you own a factory, and if you did own one when they came to power you were shot. Fascists often refrained from nationalizing a factory, but if you as the alleged owner didn't do as you were told, you were shot. Under either system, real ownership was in the hands of the omnipotent State, regardless of what any scrap of legal title paper said.

The myth of "common ownership" only muddies the issue. Public parks are thought of as held in common ("the people's property"), but that really means that the government owns them, the taxpayers pay the bill, and the public gets to use them according to the rules established and enforced by the government. Some have argued that the post office is another example of common ownership. That would mean that theoretically, each American owns about one-three-hundred-and-twenty-millionth of it, but show up at the counter and try to redeem your share and you might be surprised how fast the response can be.

From the remote but fascinating country of Mongolia comes an ownership story told to me by the country's current president (as of 2015), Elbegdorj Tsakhia, known by his friends as "EB." He earlier served as Prime Minister twice, and visited me in Michigan between those terms. I asked him during that visit what he was most proud of having accomplished as PM. He said, "I privatized Mongolia's 25 million yaks."

Yaks are large, furry cattle. For decades under communist rule, the poor creatures were owned by the government, which claimed they were "the people's property." Their total population hardly budged from the 1920s to the 1990s. E.B. decided that yaks were not a core function of government so he worked up a formula whereby all of them would be sold to the individual herdsmen. Three years later he was Prime Minister the second time. I visited him in his office in the capital of Ulan Bator and asked him, "What's the latest on the yaks?" Excitedly, he replied, "Remember when I told you we had 25 million for seven decades? Well, now we have 32 million!"

When it's *your* personal yak, not "everybody's" yak, wonderful things happen. You have a personal interest in the investment, in the capital value of the asset. You take care of the yak and make more yaks, which you then "share" with more and more people in an endless stream of peaceful, mutually beneficial trades of yak products.

Progressives yak a lot about sharing but you can't share it if you don't produce it and take care of it in the first place. Private, personal ownership of material things we create and trade for is unsurpassed as a source of the wealth that progressives want to take and "share."

Moreover, we should ask ourselves, "Is it really 'sharing' if I have to do it at gunpoint?" I was always taught that sharing was an act of free will. When you give half your sandwich to a friend who forgot to pack his lunch, you've shared it. If he threatens to beat you up if you don't give it to him, "sharing" is no longer the operative term.

So when it comes to this thing we call "ownership," it's either you or somebody else. Who should own your retirement savings—you or the government? Who should own your health-care dollars—you, the government, or some third-party payer you'd prefer to avoid? Who should decide where your child goes to school—you the parent or a handful of *other* parents different from you only by virtue of the fact that they work for the government? Who should decide what charitable activities you support—you or some congressman or bureaucrat who prefers the social welfare department over the Red Cross or your local church?

Those questions should not be answered solely on utilitarian grounds. In a free society, Person A might choose a better school or make a better investment than Person B—a fact that can't be known for certain in advance. But in any event, that does not mystically grant Person B the right to make Person A's choices for him. If freedom means anything, it means the *right* to make your own choices even if you make what others regard as mistakes. When someone argues that we cannot allow people more choices over their retirement, health care, or schools, we should demand they tell us by what right do they make these decisions for us?

Make no mistake about it: the more someone else controls you or the important decisions that govern your life or the material things that sustain it, the more they own *you*. We used to call that slavery and no gauzy, self-righteous calls to "share it" made it any less inhumane.

If you're a principled and articulate defender of private ownership of property, be ready for some progressive social engineer to lay a guilt trip on you if he thinks you're not "sharing" enough. I suspect that the preponderance of progressives will not be satisfied until their coercion-based policies effectively own the rest of us lock, stock, and barrel.

Own or be owned. Take your pick.

(Editor's Note: An earlier version of this essay appeared in the July/ August 2005 issue of The Freeman *under the title, "To Own or Be Owned: That is the Question.")*

SUMMARY

- Progressives are two-faced when it comes to ownership. They are suspicious of it when it's private and personal but supportive when it's politicized and centrally-directed
- Whether it's people or property, it will be owned. It's just a matter of whether it's owned by those to whom it belongs or those who simply want to claim it for some alleged higher cause
- Private ownership of property is both a virtue and a necessity. Get rid of it and you flush civilization down with it
- "Common ownership" is largely impractical and meaningless, even destructive

17

"ALL WE NEED IS THE RIGHT PEOPLE TO RUN THE GOVERNMENT"

By Melvin D. Barger

IT'S BEEN A TIME-HONORED PRACTICE IN AMERICA TO "THROW THE RASCALS OUT" when things go wrong in government. Supposedly this is merely the political version of what happens when the manager of a losing baseball team is replaced, or the chief executive officer of a failing corporation gets the axe.

Nobody should dispute the fact that government operations require capable, experienced people who know how to do their jobs. We've all probably had unpleasant bouts with incompetent public officials and clerks, and we wish they could be replaced.

But when government expands beyond its rightful limits, problems arise that have little to do with the competence and abilities of its officials and employees. The delusion that these problems can be solved by replacing officials only delays the day when people face the hard questions about what government should do and should not do.

Thanks to the relentless expansion of government, however, these questions are being asked the world over, with surprising solutions in some cases. There is growing criticism of government operations and regulations. There is also a rush to "privatize" many services. Though privatization moves are being made for economic reasons rather than to restore liberty, they still appear as hopeful signs.

The most important reason for limiting government to its rightful peacekeeping functions is to preserve and promote liberty. If this is done, people working singly or in groups will eventually find wonderful ways of dealing with the many human problems that government promises to solve, and meeting the human needs that government promises to meet. But as we now know, problems and needs continue to grow while the government colossus has created dangers, such as mountainous public debt and group conflicts that threaten us all and seem beyond solution. These problems worsen no matter who seems to be running things in government. Even people who used to have almost religious faith in the powers of government are becoming disillusioned as its clay feet become more exposed.

A second dilemma with excessive government is that it must always be run bureaucratically. Bureaucracy can be a maddening thing for people who have been accustomed to the speed and efficiency of market-driven services. When confronted with bureaucratic actions that displease us we tend to blame the officials in charge and call for their replacement.

But unless the officials we want replaced are completely incompetent, rooting them out is usually a waste of time and effort. As Ludwig von Mises explained many years ago, bureaucracy is neither good nor bad. Bureaucratic management is the method applied in the conduct of administrative affairs the result of which has no cash value on the market, though it may have other values to society. It is management bound to comply with detailed rules and regulations fixed by an authoritative body. "The task of the bureaucrat is to perform what these rules and regulations order him to do," Mises explained. "His discretion to act according to his own best conviction is seriously restricted by them."

Thus bureaucracy is good (and inevitable, but easily excessive, and even ridiculous and unresponsive much of the time) when it is applied in public operations such as police departments, military forces, and records bureaus. But it becomes oppressive and deadly when it is imposed on business enterprises and other human activities. As Mises shrewdly saw, the evil in bureaucracy was not in the method itself. "What many people nowadays consider an evil is not bureaucracy as such," he pointed out, "but the expansion of the sphere in which bureaucratic management is applied."

Mises then contrasted this bureaucratic system with business management or profit management, which is management directed by the profit motive. Managers, driven by the need to stay profitable (which is to say, to keep costs below income), can be given wide discretion with a minimum amount of rules and regulations. And customers will quickly let them know whether the business is providing proper goods and services and prices which customers consider favorable.

This profit-driven system has its opponents, of course, and this creates problems and frictions for entrepreneurs who want to compete for our business. Some opponents fear the new competition, while others deplore the entrepreneurs' use of resources. And one of the most effective ways of hampering entrepreneurs is to put them under either limited or total government regulation and control—that is, replacing profit-driven management with at least some degree of bureaucratic management.

So what we have in today's world is a great deal of government with additional regulation and control of private business. There is lots of grumbling about the fact that "the system doesn't seem to be working," but nobody is likely to fix it. At election time, glib office-seekers promise to reform the system and "get the country moving again." This doesn't happen, and general dissatisfaction is growing.

And there still seems to be a persistent delusion that "putting the right person in charge" will fix the problem. One favorite government response, when conditions worsen in an area, is to appoint a "czar" with special powers to bring everything together with businesslike efficiency. We have had numerous "czars" to control energy and prices, and one was recently named to deal with health reform. However highly touted, these czars soon turn out to be no more effective than the Russian rulers who gave rise to the term.

Another common fallacy, a favorite idea with pro-business political administrations, is that government operations will work better if capable business executives are found to head them. But as Mises perceptively noted, "A former entrepreneur who is given charge of a government bureau is in this capacity no longer a businessman but a bureaucrat. His objective can no longer be profit (generating more value than cost), but compliance with the rules and regulations. As head of a bureau he may have the power to alter some minor rules and some matters of internal procedure. But the setting of the bureau's activities is determined by rules and regulations which are beyond his reach."

Some people thrive in this sort of work and turn out to be excellent bureaucrats. They are the right people to run government operations when government is limited to its rightful peacekeeping functions. But if our purpose is to preserve and promote liberty while seeking the benefits of a market-driven economy, we'll look in vain for reasonable answers and solutions from government—no matter who runs it. We are slowly learning this lesson, though at great cost. We should, of course, continue to follow the time-honored American practice of "throwing the rascals out" when elected officials are performing badly. But in today's world, the officials we're criticizing might not be rascals at all, but just conscientious people trying to do jobs that shouldn't have been created in the first place.

(Editor's Note: This essay by Ohio-based businessman and writer Melvin D. Barger appeared in the 1994 edition of FEE's book, Clichés of Politics, *edited by former FEE trustee Mark Spangler. His citations of Ludwig von Mises all come from Mises's 1945 book,* Bureaucracy.*)*

SUMMARY

- As government grows, it creates more and more problems that are systemic and intractable
- Profit management and bureaucratic management are two very different things. The former seeks to generate more

value than cost while the top priority of the latter is the promulgation and implementation of rules and regulations

- The bigger government becomes, the more calls you hear endlessly for "reform," which may suggest there's something inherently defective about the political system that prevents its practitioners from ever getting things right from the start
- Running government "like a business" is a popular rhetorical point but essentially an illusion that fails to recognize the deep differences between profit-driven business and rule-driven government

18

"HUMANITY CAN BE BEST UNDERSTOOD IN A COLLECTIVE CONTEXT"

By Lawrence W. Reed

THERE ARE TWO BASIC PRISMS THROUGH WHICH WE CAN SEE, STUDY, AND PRESCRIBE for human society: individualism and collectivism. These worldviews are as different as night and day. They create a great divide in the social sciences because the perspective from which you see the world will set your thinking down one intellectual path or another.

Advocates of personal and economic freedom are usually in the individualism camp, whereas those who think of themselves these days as "progressives" are firmly in the camp of collectivism.

I think of it as the difference between snowstorms and snowflakes. A collectivist sees humanity as a snowstorm, and that's as up-close as he gets if he's consistent. An individualist sees the storm too, but is immediately drawn to the uniqueness of each snowflake that composes it. The distinction is fraught with profound implications.

No two snowstorms are alike, but a far more amazing fact is that no two snowflakes are identical either—at least so far as painstaking research has indicated. Wilson Alwyn Bentley of Jericho, Vermont, one of the first known snowflake photographers, developed a process in 1885 for capturing them on black velvet before they melted. He snapped pictures of about 5,000 of them and never found two that were the same—nor has anyone else ever since. Scientists believe that changes in humidity, temperature, and other conditions prevalent as flakes form and fall make it highly unlikely that any one flake has ever been precisely duplicated. (Ironically, Bentley died of pneumonia in 1931 after walking six miles in a blizzard. Lesson: One flake may be harmless, but a lot of them can be deadly.)

Contemplate this long enough and you may never see a snowstorm (or humanity) the same way again.

Dr. Anne Bradley is vice president of economic initiatives at the Institute for Faith, Work & Economics. At a 2013 seminar in Naples, Florida, she explained matters this way:

> When we look at a snowstorm from a distance, it looks like indistinguishable white dots peppering the sky, one blending into the next. When we get an up-close glimpse, we see how intricate, beautiful, and dissimilar each and every snowflake is. This is helpful when thinking about humans. From a distance, a large crowd of people might look the same, and it's true that we possess many similar characteristics. But we know that a more focused inspection brings us nearer to the true nature of what we're looking at. It reveals that each of us bears a unique set of skills, talents, ambitions, traits, and propensities unmatched anywhere on the planet.

This uniqueness is critical when we make policy decisions and offer prescriptions for society as a whole; for even though we each look the same in certain respects, we are actually so different, one to the next, that our sameness can only be a secondary consideration.

The late Roger J. Williams, author of *You Are Extra-Ordinary* and *Free and Unequal: The Biological Basis of Individual Liberty,* was a noted biochemistry professor at the University of Texas at Austin. He argued that fingerprints are but one of endless biological characteristics unique to each of us, including the contours and operation of our brains, nerve receptors, and circulatory systems.

These facts offer biological bases for the many other differences between one person and the next. Einstein, Williams noted, was an extremely precocious student of mathematics, but he learned language so slowly that his parents were concerned about his learning to talk. Williams summed it well more than 40 years ago when he observed, "Our individuality is as inescapable as our humanity. If we are to plan for people, we must plan for individuals, because that's the only kind of people there are."

Proceeding one step further, we must recognize that only individuals plan. When collectives are said to "plan" (e.g., "The nation plans to go to war"), it always reduces to certain, specific, identifiable individuals making plans for other individuals. The only good answer to the collectivist question, "What does America eat for breakfast?" is this: "Nothing. However, about 320 million individual Americans often eat breakfast. Many of them sometimes skip it, and on any given day, there are 320 million distinct answers to this question."

Collectivist thinking is simply not very deep or thorough. Collectivists see the world the way the nearly-blind cartoon character Mr. Magoo did—as one big blur. But unlike Mr. Magoo, they're not funny. They homogenize people in a communal blender, sacrificing the discrete features that make us who we are. The collectivist "it takes a village" mentality assigns thoughts and opinions to amorphous groups, when, in fact, only particular people hold thoughts and opinions.

Collectivists devise one-size-fits-all schemes and care little for how those schemes may affect the varied plans of real people. Any one flake means little or nothing to the collectivist because he rarely looks at them; and in any event, he implicitly dismisses the flakes because there are so many to play with. Collectivists are usually reluctant to celebrate the achievements of individuals per se because they really believe that, to quote President Obama, "you didn't build that."

Take individuals out of the equation and you take the humanity out of whatever you're promoting. What you'd never personally inflict on your neighbor, one on one, you might happily sanction if you think it'll be carried out by some faceless, collective entity to some amorphous blob on behalf of some nebulous "common good." The inescapable fact is that we are not interchangeable. Cogs in a machine are, but people most emphatically are not.

If this point is lost on you, then watch the 1998 DreamWorks animated film "Antz." The setting is an ant colony in which all ants are expected to behave as an obedient blob. This is very convenient for the tyrant ants in charge, each of which possesses a very unique personality indeed. The debilitating collectivist mindset is shaken by a single ant who marches to a different drummer—namely, his own self—and ultimately saves the colony through his individual initiative.

Karl Marx was a collectivist. Mother Theresa was an individualist. One dealt with people in lumps. The other one treated them as individuals. The lessons in that clear-cut dichotomy are legion. They are ignored only at great peril.

So what does humanity look like to you—a snowstorm or snowflakes?

If your answer is the latter, then you understand what the philosopher and historian Isaiah Berlin meant when he wrote in 1958, "But to manipulate men, to propel them toward goals which you—the social reformers—see, but they may not, is to deny their human essence, to treat them as objects without wills of their own, and therefore to degrade them."

SUMMARY

- If you see the world as a collective lump of humanity, you'll likely come to very different conclusions about life and economics than if you see it as composed of billions of unique individuals
- A snowstorm is only as big as its individual snowflakes are numerous

- Abstractions are just that, while individuals are real
- Take individuals out of the equation and you remove humans from humanity

19

"BIG GOVERNMENT IS A CHECK ON BIG BUSINESS"

By Julian Adorney

A MYTH RUNS THROUGH MOST OF AMERICA TODAY, AND IT GOES LIKE THIS: BIG business hates government and yearns for an unregulated market. But the reality is the opposite: big government can be highly profitable for big business.

Many regulations restrict competition that would otherwise challenge existing firms. At the same time, government institutions such as the Export-Import Bank—many created during the New Deal—funnel money to the largest corporations.

When government regulates X industry, it imposes high costs that hurt smaller firms and reduce competition. Imagine that the Department of Energy imposes a new rule that dishwashers must be more energy-efficient. Coming up with designs, retrofitting factories to produce these energy-efficient models, and navigating the forms and licenses around this rule might cost a dishwasher-producing firm thousands of dollars. An industry giant, with more revenue and sizeable profit margins, can absorb this cost. A small dishwasher factory that's only a year or two old, with little revenue and less profit, cannot. The latter would have to shut down. That means less competition for the industry giant, enabling it to grow even bigger and seize even more market share.

Barriers to entry, such as expensive licenses, also cripple startups and reduce competition. The progressive *New Republic* speaks favorably of how Dwolla, an Iowa-based start-up that processes payments and competes with credit card agencies, had to pay $200,000 for a license to operate. Rather than hire employees or build a better product to compete with its entrenched competition, Dwolla was forced to spend its first $200,000 on a permission slip. Dwolla could afford it; but how many less-well-funded competitors were forced from the market? How many were deterred from even starting a payment-processing business by this 6-figure barrier to entry?

For big businesses, which often sacrifice agility for size, smaller competitors are a major threat. By limiting smaller competition, government helps the industry giants at the expense of everyone else. Barriers to entry can kill the next innovative firm before it can become a threat to its giant competition. And, when this happens, we don't even know it: the killed-before-it-can-live company is a classic example of the "unseen" costs of regulation.

While regulations minimize competition, government entities subsidize big business. The Export-Import Bank, established in 1934 as part of the New Deal, exists to subsidize exports by US-based firms. The primary beneficiaries: large corporations. From 2009 to 2014, for instance, the Ex-Im Bank financed over one-quarter of Boeing's planes. Farm bills, a key element of the New Deal that still exist today, subsidize huge farms at the expense of smaller ones. The program uses a variety of methods, from crop insurance to direct payments, to subsidize farmers. The program is ostensibly designed to protect small farmers. But 75 percent of total subsidies—$126 billion from 2004 to 2013—go to the biggest 10 percent of farming companies. The program taxes consumers to funnel money to large farms.

Nor are these programs unique. National Journalism Center graduate Tim Carney argues that, "The history of big business is one of cooperation with big government." In the time of Teddy Roosevelt, big meat packers lobbied *for* federal meat inspection, knowing that the costs around compliance would crush their smaller competitors. New Deal legislation was only passed with help from the national Chamber of Commerce and the American Bankers Association. The Marshall Plan, which subsidized the sale of billions of dollars of goods to Europe, was implemented by a committee of businessmen. President Johnson created the Transportation Department in 1966, overcoming resistance from shipping interests by agreeing to exempt them from the new rules. Costly regulations for thee, but not for me.

If progressives want to see what free enterprise looks like, they need only look at the Internet. For the past twenty years, it's been largely unregulated. The result? Start-ups erupt and die every year. New competitors like Facebook bring down existing giants like MySpace, and are in turn challenged by a wealth of social media competitors. Yahoo! was the internet search king until two college kids founded Google. Google has been recently accused of monopoly status, but competitors spring up every day.

Let's imagine if the Internet—a playground of creative destruction—had been as subject to big government as brick and mortar businesses. Yahoo! would have been subsidized. Facebook would have had to pay six figures to get a licensing fee, crushing college kid Zuckerberg before he got started and preserving MySpace's market dominance. Businesses that learned to play the lobbying game would have been allowed to write regulations to crush their competitors.

For those who doubt, the proof of business' collusion with big government is in the pudding. In 2014, a surprising number of libertarian-leaning men and women are in Congress. How has big business responded? K Street has spent millions of dollars working to replace laissez-faire advocates with those who are establishment-friendly. Sadly, cronyist businesses are fighting to keep free market advocates out of power.

A final note: I have criticized progressives here, but the institution of big government, which enables businesses to hire lobbyists to write regulations or give themselves a subsidy, is the primary problem. The bigger government grows, the more powerful a tool it becomes for business prone to use it for private advantage. That's not capitalism, it's what one economist (Gene Epstein of *Barron's*) properly labeled "crapitalism."

SUMMARY

- Big Government and Big Business often play well together, at the expense of startups, little guys, and consumers
- Artificial, politically-instigated barriers to entry make markets less competitive and dynamic, and established firms more monopolistic
- A free market (true capitalism, not its adulterated "crapitalism" version) maximizes competition and therefore, service to the consumer

20

"GOVERNMENT CAN BE A COMPASSIONATE ALTERNATIVE TO THE HARSHNESS OF THE MARKETPLACE"

BY LAWRENCE W. REED

IN EVERY ELECTION CAMPAIGN, WE HEAR THE WORD "COMPASSION" AT LEAST A thousand times. One political party supposedly has it, the other one doesn't. Big government programs are evidence of compassion; cutting back government is a sign of cold-hearted meanness. By their misuse of the term for partisan advantage, partisans and ideologues have thoroughly muddied up the real meaning of the word.

The fact is that some of what is labeled "compassionate" is just that, and it does a world of good; but a whole lot of what is labeled "compassionate" is nothing of the sort, and it does a world of harm. The former tends to be very personal in nature while the latter imposes involuntary burdens on others.

As Marvin Olasky pointed out in his 1994 book, *The Tragedy of American Compassion*, the original definition of compassion as noted in *The Oxford English Dictionary* is "suffering together with another, participation in suffering." The emphasis, as the word itself shows— "com," which means *with*, and "passion," from the Latin term "pati," meaning *to suffer*—is on personal involvement with the needy, suffering *with* them, not just giving to them. Noah Webster, in the 1834 edition of his *American Dictionary of the English Language*, similarly defined compassion as "a suffering with another."

But the way most people use the term today is a corruption of the original. It has come to mean little more than, as Olasky put it, "the feeling, or emotion, when a person is moved by the suffering or distress of another, and by the desire to relieve it." There is a world of difference between those two definitions: One demands personal action, the other simply a "feeling" that usually is accompanied by a call for someone else—namely, *government*—to deal with the problem. One describes a Red Cross volunteer, the other describes the typical progressive demagogue who gives away little or nothing of his own resources but lots of yours.

The plain fact is that government compassion is not the same as personal and private compassion. When we expect the government to substitute for what we ourselves ought to do, we expect the impossible and we end up with the intolerable. We don't really solve problems, we just manage them expensively into perpetuity and create a bunch of new ones along the way.

From 1965, the beginning of the so-called War on Poverty, to 1994, total welfare spending in the United States was $5.4 trillion in constant 1993 dollars. In 1965, total government welfare spending was just over 1 percent of gross domestic product, but by 1993 it had risen to 5.1 percent of GDP annually—higher than the record set during the Great Depression. The poverty rate, which had been steadily declining before the Great Society, thirty years later was almost exactly where it was in 1965. It was apparent when "welfare reform" was enacted in 1996 that millions on welfare were living lives of demoralizing dependency; families were rewarded for breaking up; and the number of children born out of wedlock was in the stratosphere—terrible facts brought about, in large part, by "compassionate" government programs.

A person's willingness to spend government funds on aid programs is not evidence that the person himself is compassionate. Professor William

B. Irvine of Wright State University in Dayton, Ohio, once explained: "It would be absurd to take a person's willingness to increase defense spending as evidence that the person is himself brave, or to take a person's willingness to spend government money on athletic programs as evidence that the person is himself physically fit. In the same way as it is possible for a couch potato to favor government funding of athletic teams, it is possible for a person who lacks compassion to favor various government aid programs; and conversely, it is possible for a compassionate person to oppose these programs."

It is a mistake to use a person's political beliefs as the litmus test of his compassion. Professor Irvine said that if you want to determine how compassionate an individual is, you are wasting your time if you ask for whom he voted; instead, you should ask what charitable contributions he has made and whether he has done any volunteer work lately. You might also inquire into how he responds to the needs of his relatives, friends, and neighbors.

Many of the political world's most boisterous welfare statists are also among the most duplicitous and selfish (in the bad sense of the term) hypocrites. While small-government conservatives and libertarians usually give generously from their own pockets, charitable organizations are often lucky to get a little more than token donations from the "progressive" welfare statists of the world. For a mountain of evidence in that regard, see the 2006 book, *Who Really Cares?* by Arthur Brooks, then at Syracuse University and now president of the American Enterprise Institute.

It's worth noting that not even progressives donate to supposedly "compassionate" government agencies a penny more than the law requires them to. There's nothing illegal about writing out a check to the "Department of Health and Human Services" but progressives, when they seek to personally help others, tend to write their checks out to private agencies. Government agencies almost never receive "donations."

True compassion is a bulwark of strong families and communities, of liberty and self-reliance, while the false compassion of the second usage is fraught with great danger and dubious results. True compassion is people helping people out of a genuine sense of caring and brotherhood. It is not asking your legislator or congressman to do it for you. True compassion comes from your heart, not from the state or federal treasury. True compassion is a deeply personal thing, not a check from a distant bureaucracy.

In a television interview in Nassau, Bahamas in November 2012, I was asked by host Wendall Jones, "Mr. Reed, what about the Good Samaritan in the New Testament? Doesn't that story show that government should help people?" My reply: "Wendall, what made the Good Samaritan good was the fact that he personally helped the stricken man along the road. If he had simply told the helpless chap to ring up his congressman, no one to this day would have the gall to call him anything but a good-for-nothing."

"But what about Christianity itself?" Jones then asked me. "Isn't it in favor of redistribution as a compassionate way to help the poor?" Fortunately, I know a few things about the Bible and Christianity. My reply: "Wendall, the Eighth Commandment says 'Thou shalt not steal.' It doesn't say, 'Thou shalt not steal unless the other guy has more than you do or unless you're convinced that you can spend it better or unless you can find a politician to take it on your behalf.' And even more to the point, a new book on the subject, *For the Least of These: A Biblical Answer to Poverty*, answers this in both a detailed and scholarly fashion.

Progressives are often so convinced of their moral superiority that they tend to be very intolerant of a good, opposing argument. Mr. Jones edited out the above exchange before airing the show but you can see the rest by searching on YouTube for "Lawrence W. Reed on the Platform, Nassau N.P. Bahamas."

The marketplace is often dismissed as a cold, impersonal and selfish place where compassion takes a back seat to self-interest. But that view ignores some important facts: 1) The marketplace is what produces the wealth that compassion allows you to share or give away; 2) Historically, the freest of societies are the most compassionate in the truest sense of the term; 3) Nothing about being a government employee spending other people's money makes you more compassionate or effective than the rest of society; 4) Government "compassion" usually gets diverted towards vote-buying and programs that perpetuate the very problems it was supposed to remedy. The news brings daily reminders that there's no shortage of "harshness" in government—as well as greed, waste, fraud and inefficiency.

The next time you hear the word "compassion," probe the person invoking it to find out if he really knows what he's talking about—or at least to determine if he does it with his own resources.

(Editor's Note: Earlier versions of this essay have appeared in FEE publications under the title, "What is Real Compassion?")

SUMMARY

- "Compassion" isn't simply giving something away, especially if what you're giving wasn't yours in the first place
- True compassion means getting personally involved
- Instinctively, when we want to help others with our own time and resources, we overwhelmingly tend to do so through donations of time and money to private agencies, not to public ones
- The marketplace, where self-interest is a powerful motivator for the creation of wealth, is therefore the primary source for whatever wealth anybody has to give away

21

"CAPITALISM'S SWEATSHOPS AND CHILD LABOR CRY OUT FOR GOVERNMENT INTERVENTION"

By Paul L. Poirot

PREVALENT IN THE UNITED STATES AND OTHER INDUSTRIALIZED COUNTRIES IS THE belief that without governmental intervention, such as wage and hour legislation, child labor laws, and rules concerning working conditions for women, the long hours and grueling conditions of the "sweatshop" would run rampant.

The implication is that legislators, in the days of Abraham Lincoln, for instance, were cruel and inconsiderate of the poor—no better than the caricatured factory owners of the times who would employ men and women and children at low wages, long hours, and poor working conditions. Otherwise, had they been humanitarians, legislators of a century ago and earlier would have prohibited child labor, legislated a forty-hour week, and passed other laws to improve working conditions.

But the simple truth is that legislators of a few generations ago in the United States were powerless, as Mao or Nehru or Chavez or Castro have been powerless in more recent times, to wave a wand of restrictionist legislation and thereby raise the level of living and abolish poverty among the people. If such a miracle were possible, every dictator and every democratically chosen legislator would "push the button" without hesitation.

The reason why women and children no longer find it necessary to work for low wages under poor conditions from dawn to dusk six days or more a week is the same reason why strong healthy men can avoid such onerous labor in a comparatively free industrialized society: surviving and earning a living are made easier through the use of tools and capital accumulated by personal savings and investment.

In fiction, the children of nature may dwell in an earthly paradise; but in the real life of all primitive societies, the men and women and all the children struggle constantly against the threat of starvation. Such agrarian economies support all the people they can, but with high infant mortality and short life spans for all survivors.

When savings can be accumulated, then tools can be made and life's struggle somewhat eased as industrialization begins. And with the growth of savings and tools and production and trade, the population may increase. As incomes rise and medical practices improve, children stand a better chance of survival, and men and women may live longer with less effort. Not that savings are accumulated rapidly or that industrialization occurs overnight; it is a long, slow process. And in its early stages, the surviving women and children are likely to be found improving their chances as best they can by working in factories and so-called sweatshops. To pass a law prohibiting such effort at that stage of development of the society would simply be to condemn to death a portion of the expanding population. *To prohibit child labor in Third World countries today would be to condemn millions to starvation.*

Once a people have developed habits of industry and thrift, learned to respect life and property, discovered how to invest their savings in creative and productive and profitable enterprise, found the mainspring of human progress—then, and only then, after the fact of industrialization and a prosperous expanding economy, is it possible to enact child labor laws without thereby passing a death sentence.

A wise and honest humanitarian will know that poverty (and worse) lurks behind every minimum wage law that sets a wage higher than some individual is capable of earning; behind every compulsory 40-hour week rule that catches a man with a family he can't support except through more than 40 hours of effort; behind every legislated condition of employment that forces some marginal employer into bankruptcy, thus destroying the job opportunities he otherwise afforded; behind every legal action that virtually compels retirement at age 65.

Men will take their children and women out of sweatshops as fast as they can afford it—as fast as better job opportunities develop—as fast as the supply of capital available per worker increases. The only laws necessary for that purpose are those which protect life and private property and thus encourage personal saving and investment.

To believe that labor laws are the cause of improved living and working conditions, rather than an after-thought, leads to harmful laws that burden wealth creation, sap the incentive of the energetic, and close the doors of opportunity to those least able to afford it. And the ultimate effect is not a boon to mankind but a major push back toward barbarism.

(*Editor's Note: This essay is slightly edited from the original, published in* The Freeman *in 1963 under the title "To Abolish Sweatshops."*)

SUMMARY

- Sweatshops and child labor were commonplace in pre-industrial, pre-capitalist days because production and productivity were so low, not because people disliked their wives and children more than they do today
- Savings, investment and economic growth improve working and economic conditions faster and more assuredly than well-intentioned but misguided laws that simply close doors of opportunity

22

"VOLUNTARY, MARKET-BASED ARRANGEMENTS 'USE' PEOPLE"

By Gary M. Galles

AMONG THE MOST WELL-WORN MORAL CRITICISMS OF VOLUNTARY ARRANGEMENTS is that they treat people as things or commodities, rather than as individuals. In other words, market arrangements are indicted because participants "use" people in the process. As the late economist Paul Heyne described it, "such a system seems somehow to violate our profound moral conviction that nothing is more valuable than individual persons, and that each person ought to be treated as a unique end, never as a means to some further end."

The irony is that those who understand and respect market arrangements do so precisely because "nothing is more valuable than individual persons." I echo FEE's founder Leonard Read's understanding that "An individualist…looks upon society as the upshot, outcome, effect, recapitulation incidental to what is valued above all else, namely, each distinctive individual human being." But why have such anti-individual criticisms persisted so long, despite the contradiction? In part, due to a rhetorical bait-and-switch that changes the meaning of "use" in the middle of the argument.

There is widespread moral condemnation of "using" people. However, use has different meanings. Use can mean utilize or employ, with no implication of harm to others. That is what we mean when we say someone uses a hammer. It is also what happens when people voluntarily provide their services to advance others' purposes in markets. In contrast, use can also mean abuse or harm, particularly as a result of force or fraud. That is what we mean when we say "you pretended to care about me, but you were just using me."

The first meaning is consistent with either imposing no harm on others or benefitting them (as in mutually acceptable market arrangements, which individuals would not otherwise enter into); the second meaning requires that others are harmed. And changing the meaning from the first to the second in midstream allows a logical cheat.

Some people may be fooled by saying, "You use others in markets; using people harms them." But that is far less likely if you clarify which "use" you mean. "You utilized others' willingly supplied services, therefore you harmed them" will convince far fewer. So language misuse, abetted by sloppy thinking, can transform the reality of mutual benefits from uncoerced market exchanges into the fiction of exploitation theory.

There is another logical problem that arises from saying we should treat people as ends in themselves and never as means. It is not a choice between the two, because they are not mutually exclusive. People are both ends in themselves and the means by which others advance their ends.

What others offer us in all mutually agreed-to exchanges are means to better advance our ends. But to treat people's actions or services as means to our ends does not demean them as individuals; it is simply inherent in mutual benefit. And to miss that distinction, condemning such arrangements as the unethical use of others, comes very close to the self-contradictory assertion that nothing mutually beneficial is allowable. Instead, we should laud rather than lambaste a system that can dovetail the often incompatible plans and purposes of multitudes of different individuals to expand what can actually be achieved.

Further, when people freely choose their arrangements, each respects others as important ends in themselves in an important way that is absent when others dictate what is allowable. It allows them their freedom, based in self-ownership, to choose how best to use the means they have at their disposal.

Mutually voluntary arrangements are those the participants believe best advance their ability to achieve their ends, without violating others' similar ability. Nothing is detracted from the ability to pursue the ends we each choose; possibilities for both are expanded. How can we better advance others' ends than letting them choose how to use their current means most productively as they see it? As Philip Wicksteed wrote over a century ago in *The Common Sense of Political Economy*, voluntary economic relations ease "the limitations...of their own direct resources...by the very act that brings a corresponding liberation to those with whom they deal...[leaving] no room to bring against it the charge of being intrinsically sordid and degrading."

The hypothetical ideal of always treating people as objects of benevolence rather than utilizing their services through mutually beneficial exchanges is also unattainable. As Philip Wicksteed put it, "The limitation of our powers would prevent our taking an equally active interest in everyone's affairs." In any society larger than an immediate family, we simply cannot know enough to organize relationships based on benevolence.

Consider the sheer number of transactions and transactors involved in our economic arrangements. As Leonard Read's famous "I, Pencil" essay demonstrated, vast numbers are involved for even the simplest products, much less more complex products, such as automobiles. In such circumstances, the alternatives are not coordinating relationships via exchange (another name for persuasion) or via charity, but between coordinating relationships via exchange or coordinating them far less well, if at all, because it exceeds our knowledge and capabilities.

Paul Heyne summarized it well:

> When money prices, rather than concern for each other as
> persons, coordinate social transactions, social cooperation
> becomes possible on a more extensive scale. Those who would
> like to force all social transactions into the personal mode do
> not realize how much of what they now take for granted
> would become wholly impossible in the world of their ide-
> als...They are ignoring the incredible complexity of the sys-
> tem of social cooperation by means of which we are fed,
> clothed, housed, warned, healed, transported, comforted,
> entertained, challenged, inspired, educated and generally
> served.

Claims that market arrangements involve the unethical "using" of
others are of lengthy pedigree. But they are also of questionable merit.
They rhetorically transform the utilization of other individuals' services
in ways that benefit all parties involved into "using" others to their
imagined detriment. They treat the issue as a choice between treating
others as means or as ends, when honoring others as ends in themselves,
and so according them the dignity of choosing how best to accomplish
their purposes, leads them to voluntarily provide the means to advance
others' ends. The employ a standard of always treating people as objects
of benevolence rather than utilizing their services through mutually
beneficial exchanges, assuming other things equal, when trying to do so
would destroy many of the forms of social cooperation that voluntary
arrangements have produced so dependably that we rely on them daily.

However, careful thinking, not cowed or manipulated by misleading
arguments, leads to diametrically opposed conclusions. If we accept the
premise that individuals and their development are our ultimate ends,
the voluntary arrangements they evolve are, as Friedrich Hayek pointed
out, among society's greatest creations, not its nemesis.

SUMMARY

- Advocates of free markets have long been accused of supporting arrangements that "use" people. It's ironic because free markets are the one economic arrangement that most respects and empowers individuals!
- Markets, because they are rooted in the free choice of individuals, self-ownership, voluntary and contractual relationships and customer satisfaction, are far less likely to "use" people (in the pejorative sense) than arrangements that are coerced, centrally planned or bureaucratic
- People should not be treated as objects of benevolence, but rather, as sovereign individuals with whom we deal voluntarily, peacefully and for the mutual benefit that occurs through freedom of choice

23

"THE BALANCE OF TRADE DEFICIT REQUIRES GOVERNMENT ACTION"

By Lawrence W. Reed

I HAVE A DIRTY LITTLE SECRET. IT'S ABOUT A NAGGING PROBLEM I HAVE HAD FOR a long time. It just never seems to go away. Heretofore, I have not wanted to admit to this problem in public because the newspaper headlines remind me monthly that this sort of thing is bad and embarrassing. But I'm going to come clean, hoping that maybe someone out there can help me.

My problem is this: I have a trade deficit with J.C. Penney. That's right. Year after year, I buy more from J.C. Penney than J.C. Penney buys from me.

In fact, J.C. Penney has never yet bought anything at all from me. It's been a one-way street right from the day I got my credit card in the mail. And I don't expect that this is going to change any time soon because the retail chain shows no interest in buying my chief export, which is columns like this one. It just doesn't seem fair.

I've actually considered several options. Each one would probably reduce or eliminate my trade deficit with J.C. Penney, but some wise guy always points out new problems that each of these scenarios might create:

1. I could get Congress to force the company to buy enough of my articles to offset what I spend in its stores. But the more J.C. Penney buys from me, the less it will be able to buy from others, which will only increase *their* trade deficits.
2. I could get Congress to force J.C. Penney to cut its prices so that I won't have to spend as much to get what I want. I thought that might at least reduce my deficit, but at lower prices I might actually be tempted to buy more. Or J.C. Penney might come under fire from the antitrust people for dumping its goods below cost.
3. I could simply quit buying from J.C. Penney. That would really teach them a lesson. But then, doggone it, I *like* what I've been buying from them. If I boycott them, wouldn't that be like cutting off my nose to spite my face?

Of course, I don't really mean any of this. As an economist, I know that there's a fourth option here and it's the only one that makes any sense: I should ignore this "problem" and never pay any attention again to whatever the trade situation is between J.C. Penney and me, except to pay my bills on time. America as a whole should do essentially the same thing. If we fired the people in Washington, D.C. who compile the balance of trade numbers, the so-called problem will go away.

Every month, the U.S. Commerce Department releases the official "balance of trade" figures showing the difference between the value of merchandise that enters the country and the value of merchandise that leaves the country. If imports exceed exports, America has a trade *deficit*, which sets off alarm bells in Washington. If exports are greater than imports, we're all supposed to celebrate because that's a trade *surplus*.

By this logic, draining the country of all goods and accepting none from abroad would be the best possible trade news. We wouldn't be able to celebrate, however, because we'd all starve. But at least the government's books would register one heck of a trade surplus.

The balance of trade numbers, by the way, represent a very incomplete picture of trade. They attempt to measure merchandise only, but traders exchange many other things too. If a Canadian businessman sells Americans lumber, he earns dollars but he doesn't have to buy merchandise with them. He might instead invest in real estate, purchase securities (government or private), or contract for certain services. Those things don't get counted in the "balance of trade."

Progressives aren't the only ones who get hung up on this trade-deficit thing and then favor pseudo-solutions to a non-problem. It's a throwback to the less enlightened times of sixteenth-century mercantilists. They argued that a nation must never buy more from foreigners than it sells to them because that would produce an "unfavorable balance of trade" that would have to be settled by an outflow of gold or silver. The mercantilists wrongly assumed that gold and silver were the real wealth of a nation, not goods and services. They were also wrong to render value judgments about other people's trading activities. The fact is that there can be nothing "unfavorable" about voluntary trade from the point of view of the individuals actually doing the trading, otherwise they would not have engaged in it in the first place.

The principle that both sides benefit from trade is readily visible when it involves two parties within a country; it somehow becomes confused when an invisible political barrier separates the parties. Neither the mercantilists of yesteryear nor those who fuss about the trade deficit today have ever satisfactorily answered this fundamental question: Since each and every trade is "favorable" to the individual traders, how is it possible that these transactions can be totaled up to produce something "unfavorable"?

Scottish economist Adam Smith was among the first to attack the notion that exports are good and imports are bad. He postulated a "harmony of interests" in trade, by which both parties to an exchange benefit. With the exception of obvious fraudulent practices, which are minimal in number and a responsibility of the courts, there can be nothing "unfavorable" about voluntary trade *from the point of view of the individuals doing the trading,* otherwise those individuals would not have engaged in it.

To return to my initial example, I benefit when I buy from J.C. Penney or I wouldn't keep doing it. The folks at J.C. Penney benefit as well because they would rather have my money than the stuff they sell me. We're both better off because we have a trade relationship, which is why neither party ever complains about it. This would be no less true if J.C. Penney happened to be a company from Japan or Uganda.

Ultimately, the dollars that go abroad to pay for imports will come back to buy American exports. But even if they didn't—in other words, even if goods come here and dollars go there to simply stuff foreign mattresses—Americans with their supposedly harmful trade deficit would have the better end of the deal. We would get goods like electronics and automobiles, and foreigners would be stuck with slips of paper decorated with pictures of dead American politicians.

Forget the trade deficit. We should occupy ourselves with more important things, like the next sale at J.C. Penney's.

(Editor's Note:. An earlier version of this essay was published in The Freeman *in December 1998.)*

SUMMARY

- Each of us as individuals have a "balance of trade" with other individuals but none of us care about the numbers; we care about the goods and services we're trading for
- Balance of trade figures count only merchandise. They leave out a huge chunk of world trade involving other things, from real estate to securities to services
- No trades are deemed as anything but "favorable" by those engaged in the trading so how can anyone add all those trades up and arrive at something "unfavorable"?

24

"AMERICANS SQUANDER THEIR INCOMES ON THEMSELVES WHILE PUBLIC NEEDS ARE NEGLECTED"

By Edmund A. Opitz

OUR SOCIETY IS AFFLUENT, WE ARE TOLD—BUT ONLY AFFLUENT IN THE PRIVATE sector, alas! The public sector—meaning the political structure on which our society spends a third of its energy to maintain—starves. Mr. and Mrs. America bounce along in their fancy, expensive cars over bumpy highways—the best road their government can build with the limited resources permitted it. They queue up to pay scalper's prices for tickets to ball games with nary a thought that this indulgence contributes to the non-building of a political housing project in an already overcrowded city. That evening they dine at a ritzy restaurant, and government, as a result, lacks the means to supply water for a dam it has just constructed in a drought area. Americans, in short, go in big for private indulgence at the very time when the State needs their money.

Those who advance this or similar lines of criticism are perfectly correct on one point: If there is to be an increase in political spending, there must be a consequent decrease in private spending; some people must do without. The well-being of individual persons in any society varies inversely with the money at the disposal of the political class. All money spent by the governing group is taken from private citizens—who otherwise would spend it quite differently on goods of their choice. The state lives on taxes (or what it borrows now and pays back with taxes later), and taxes are a charge against the economically productive part of society.

The Opulent State, fancied by progressives who criticize the Affluent Society, cannot exist except as a result of massive interference with free choice. To establish it, a society of freely choosing individuals must yield to a society in which the lives of the many are collectively planned and controlled by the few.

The state, in our Affluent Society, already deprives us of one-third and more of our substance (in both direct and indirect taxes and the costs of regulation and compliance it imposes). Not enough! say the critics. How much then? Fifty percent? A hundred? Enough, at any rate, so that no life shall go unplanned if they can help it. This is the ancient error of authoritarianism. The planning-inclined intellectual, from time immemorial, has dreamed up ethical and esthetic standards for the rest of mankind—only to have them ignored. His efforts to persuade people to embrace them meet with scant success. The masses are too ignorant to know what is good for them, so why not impose the right ideas on them by direct political action? The state is too weak and poor? Well, make it strong and rich, he urges, and so it is done. But the state acts from political and power motives and often devours even the intellectuals who argued on its behalf.

Every society devises some public means of protecting its peaceful citizens against the violent actions of others, but this is too limiting a role for government to satisfy the critics of the so-called Affluent Society. The massive state interference they advocate is designed, they say, to protect the people from the consequences of their own folly, and the way to do this is to pass anti-folly laws to prevent wrong choices.

There are degrees of wisdom, true, and some people are downright foolish. They spend their money at the races when the roof needs repair, or they install costly television services when they're still making payments on their boat. In a free society, however, this is their right just as it is their right to say or print foolish or unpopular things. This is part of what it means to be free! The exercise of freedom invariably results in some choices that are unwise or wrong (Hey, is it any different in government?). But, by living with the consequences of his foolish choices a man learns to choose more wisely next time. Trial and error first; then, if he is free, trial and success later. But because no man is competent to manage another, persistent error and failure are built-in features of the Opulent State.

(Editor's Note: This essay first appeared in the 1962 edition of Clichés of Socialism *at a time when the fallacy it addresses was more widely proclaimed than it is today. John Kenneth Galbraith's influential 1958 book,* The Affluent Society, *largely discredited in subsequent decades, was often and favorably cited in the early 1960s. Today, with government consuming considerably more of total income than it did half a century ago, and wasting much of it, it's not so easy to argue that the public sector is being starved. That doesn't stop progressives, however, from frequently claiming in various ways that government deserves even more.)*

SUMMARY

- If the political class gets more to spend, that means that private individuals have exactly that much less to spend according to their own choices
- Authoritarianism always argues for more of what belongs to others; authoritarians never believe they have enough as long as anybody gets to make his own choices rather than having the State make those choices for him
- Freedom means spending your own money the way you choose, even if you sometimes choose foolishly. And there's nothing about government that ensures that the people in it who spend other people's money will spend it more wisely than would those who earned it in the first place

25

"IF GOVERNMENT DOESN'T RELIEVE DISTRESS, WHO WILL?"

By Leonard E. Read

PRESIDENT GROVER CLEVELAND, VETOING A CONGRESSIONAL APPROPRIATION OF $10,000 to buy seed grain for drought-stricken Texans, may have given us all the answer we need to this cliché:

> The friendliness and charity of our countrymen can always be relied upon to relieve their fellow-citizens in misfortune...Federal aid in such cases encourages the expectation of paternal care on the part of the government and weakens the sturdiness of our national character, while it prevents the indulgence among our people of that kindly sentiment and conduct which strengthens the bonds of a common brotherhood.

No doubt many of the congressmen who voted for this appropriation were sincerely asking, "If the federal government does not save these poor Texans, who will?" President Cleveland had only to veto the measure and write an explanation. But we private citizens have no power beyond reason and persuasion. What, then, might we have said? This would be one honest answer: "I am not clairvoyant and, thus, I do not know *who* will relieve these people. However, I do know that Texans acting on their own initiative and with their own resources will take care of themselves better than they will be taken care of by any number of politicians imitating Robin Hood."

The question, "If government does not relieve distress, who will?" is illogical. No one can ever answer, *who* will. Thus, the cliché-maker wins his implied point without a struggle—unless one lays claim to clairvoyance or exposes the fakery of the question. (Furthermore, implicit in the question itself is the dubious assumption that if government does it, it will be done well, efficiently and without the corruption of politics.)

Every reader of these lines can prove to himself, by reflecting on personal experiences, that the relief of distress is an unpredictable event. Time after time, each of us, with no preconception, has observed distress and then taken steps to relieve it—with his own income! *(Editor's Note: Author Marvin Olasky in his 1999 book,* The American Leadership Tradition, *notes that the private, voluntary donations that poured in to help Texas after Cleveland's veto amounted to at least ten times what the President had vetoed.)*

Prior to the 1930s, before the federal government assumed responsibility for "relief," no one could have foretold *who* would come to whose rescue; yet, since 1623, there is no record of famine or starvation in this country. Among a people where the principles of freedom were more widely practiced and government more limited than elsewhere, there has been less distress and more general well-being than history had ever recorded. Societies saddled with bureaucracy have no record of coming to the aid of free societies; it has always been the other way around.

Charity is a personal virtue. When government does not undertake coercively-funded grants-in-aid ("relief"), millions of adults stand as guardians against distress. Their available charitable energy is totally at work observing distress in its neighborly detail, judging and coming to the rescue with the fruits of the labor of each charitable person. And on occasions of major disaster, there has been a voluntary pooling of individual resources, often extravagant.

What happens when government takes over? Charity gives way to politics. Funds coercively collected are dispensed to individuals according to group, class, or occupational category. This has no semblance of charity; it is the robbery of Peter to pay Paul. Further, when government constructs a feeding trough and fills it with fruits extorted from the citizenry, it creates new claimants and aggravates the problem it set out to solve.

It is not only the so-called "relief" projects that are based on this same tired cliché, but most other cases of government intervention in our society: "If the government doesn't do the job, who will?" If the government doesn't level mountains and fill valleys, drain swamps and water deserts, build highways over waters and seaways over land, subsidize failure and penalize productivity and thrift, send men to the moon and promise the moon to mankind, and a thousand and one other projects— if the government doesn't do these things, that is, force taxpayers to do them, who will? And more often than not the answer is that probably no one in his right mind would ever think of doing such things—at his own risk, with his own money. Eventually, a time might come when some ingenious person would see a way to do one or more of these jobs, in hope of profit, and would take the chance.

But there is no way to determine in advance *who* that pioneer might be. The most that can be done is to leave men free, for only among free men do pioneers emerge. Freedom affords every opportunity, in charitable enterprises or on the market, for the best—not the worst—to rise topside.

(Editor's Note: A version of this essay first appeared in FEE's book, Clichés of Socialism, *in 1962.)*

SUMMARY

- Nobody can name the names in advance of those who might come to the aid of fellow citizens in distress. The question is illogical

- Without government assistance, a massive amount of private, voluntary aid has poured forth from American citizens since the first settlement here. Is there any reason to suppose that politicians are more caring, compassionate or effective in providing relief with other people's money than are the individuals who elected them in the first place, and who get personally involved in the relief of citizens nearby?
- Government is not true charity and it politicizes everything it touches

26

"HISTORICAL PRESERVATION WON'T HAPPEN UNLESS THE GOVERNMENT TAKES CHARGE"

By Lawrence W. Reed

"SOLD!" CRIED THE SOTHEBY'S AUCTIONEER ON THE NIGHT OF DECEMBER 18, 2007, as one of history's oldest political documents changed hands. It was the Magna Carta, or rather a copy of it that dated to 1297. The buyer was not a government but an individual, a Washington lawyer named David Rubenstein. He paid $21.3 million for it and promptly announced he wanted his newly acquired private property to stay on public view at the National Archives in the nation's capital.

A privately owned Magna Carta? Aren't such important things supposed to be public property? A couple of American students visiting Britain certainly thought so. For a story that aired on CNN about the auction at Sotheby's, they were interviewed at the British Library in London while gazing on another of the great charter's copies on display there.

"I couldn't imagine that there is still a privately owned copy of the Magna Carta floating around the world. It seems really incredible that any one person should actually have that in their possession," one of the young scholars pronounced. "Personally, I hope the government or some charitable foundation gets a hold of it so that everybody can enjoy seeing it," chimed the other. Both assumed that private property and public benefit, at least with regard to historical preservation, were incompatible.

The Magna Carta copy that Rubenstein bought will not be spirited into his closet because it is the new owner's wish that it be preserved for public display. While some might say humanity lucked out in this particular instance, it really is just the latest in a rich heritage of private care of documents, manuscripts, and objects of historical significance. Indeed, the very copy Rubenstein bought was previously owned by businessman Ross Perot's foundation, which in turn had acquired it in 1984 from yet another private owner, the Brudenell family of Britain. Given that record, those students should have sung hosannas to private efforts like that of Rubenstein's.

The content of books from the ancient world appears to have been brought into the digital age largely through private efforts. Through various eras, libraries, scribes, and printers were supported to a great extent through private patronage. Ecclesiastical institutions were critical in preserving texts that are important to the Western tradition, points out Dr. Ryan Olson of the Kern Family Foundation in Wisconsin and holder of a doctorate in the classics from Oxford University.

For example, Olson says, in the sixth century Cassiodorus finished his career as a government official in Ravenna and organized monastic efforts to copy Christian and classical texts. Some work of his monks seems to have ended up in Rome, where it could be more influential. Though the history of transmission can be difficult to trace, scholars have argued that at least one classical work, by Cato, seems to have survived to this day because of Cassiodorus's efforts. "It is our intention," Cassiodorus wrote shortly before his death, "to weave into one fabric and assign to proper usage whatever the ancients have handed down to modern custom."

I also learned from Olson that the Roman politician, lawyer, and author Cicero revealed in his letters a network of extensive personal libraries. Those private collections preserved important books that could be read by members of the public and even borrowed and sent with messengers. Books could be consulted or copied for one's own library and returned to the owner. If one wanted to look at several books, a personal visit to a private library could be arranged.

The Bodleian Library at Oxford, where Olson once studied, was founded by Sir Thomas Bodley and dedicated in 1602. King James I, on entering the library in August 1605, said its founder should be dubbed "Sir Thomas Godly." Bodley had spent his considerable personal wealth acquiring books and early manuscripts that have formed the core of one of the most extensive collections in the world. That collection includes among its innumerable treasures a first edition of *Don Quixote*, a manuscript of Confucius acquired at a time when few could read its Chinese characters, a fourteenth-century copy of Dante's *The Divine Comedy*, as well as first editions of the works of John Milton, who called the library a "most sacred centre," a "glorious treasure-house" of "the best Memorials of Man."

Additional examples of historical preservation through private means are, it turns out, legion. Pittsburgh banker Andrew Mellon acquired a massive assortment of prized artwork. He donated his entire collection (plus $10 million for construction) to start the National Gallery of Art in Washington, D.C. Tens of thousands of historic homes and buildings all across America are owned and maintained privately, many of them refurbished and open for public viewing. Even historic lighthouses, once largely public property, are being preserved today by private owners after decades of neglect by government authorities. On and on it goes.

Think about this: Private historians all over the world, every single day, are turning out articles and books that dust off bits of the past and, in a new form, put them in front of new generations of readers—preserving history in the process. The idea that government subsidies are necessary to get historians to write history is absurd.

The more one looks into this, the more apparent it is that private efforts have not just been a sideshow in historical preservation. They have been the centerpiece. And why should it be otherwise? Private owners invest their own resources, acquiring an instant and personal interest in the "capital" value of the historical asset. Being a government employee does not make one more interested in, or better equipped to care for, the things we regard as historically valuable than those many private citizens who put their own resources on the line.

By the way, have you ever noticed that the greatest book-burners in history have been governments, not private individuals?

By way of prices, markets send signals about what should be preserved and what should be discarded. The scarcer something valuable becomes, the more the price of any one of its dwindling supply will rise. That's an incentive for private parties to buy and hold, and also to exhibit if others value it enough to want to see it. Government ownership means we have to trust to bureaucrats to preserve what they don't personally own.

So what's the problem with a copy of Magna Carta being purchased by a private citizen? Nothing at all. To suggest otherwise is simply to repeat an uninformed and antiquated prejudice. In a civil society of free people, that prejudice should be rare enough to be a museum piece.

SUMMARY

- Why sell people and markets short when it comes to history? Examples are endless of private preservation and restoration
- Private efforts have not just been a sideshow in historical preservation. They have been the centerpiece
- By way of prices, markets send signals about what should be preserved and what should be discarded
- Private ownership means somebody has a direct incentive to preserve; if government owns it, we all have incentives to use and maybe even abuse something that is historically valuable. Government ownership means we have to trust to bureaucrats to preserve what they don't personally own

27

"GOVERNMENT MUST HAVE THE POWER TO MAKE PEOPLE TAKE BETTER CARE OF THEMSELVES"

By Lawrence W. Reed

A FEW MONTHS AGO, I WALKED INTO A RESTAURANT IN FLORIDA, AND SAID, "A nonsmoking table for two, please." The greeter replied, "No problem. All restaurants in Florida are nonsmoking by law. Follow me."

For a brief moment as we walked to our table, I thought to myself: "Good! No chance of even a whiff of a cigarette. I like that!"

And then I felt shame. I had fallen victim to the same statist impulse that afflicts today's so-called "progressives." For 40 years, I thought I was a passionate, uncompromising believer in the free society. Yet for a few seconds, I took pleasure in government trampling on the liberties of consenting adults in a private setting.

This incident troubled me enough to think about it a long while. I wanted to know why my first instinct was to abandon principles for a little convenience. And if a committed freedom-lover like me can be so easily tugged in the wrong direction, what does that say for ever getting nonbelievers to eschew similar or more egregious temptations?

At first, I thought about the harm that many doctors believe second-hand smoke can do. Perhaps it wasn't wrong for government to protect nonsmokers if what we have here is a case of one person imposing a harmful externality on an unwilling other. Then I quickly realized two things: no one compelled me to enter the place, and the restaurant belonged to neither the government nor me. The plain fact is that in a genuinely free society, a private owner who wants to allow some people in his establishment to smoke has as much right to permit it as you or I have to go elsewhere. It's not as though people aren't aware of the risks involved. Moreover, no one has a right to compel another citizen to provide him with a smoke-free restaurant.

Besides, I can think of a lot of risky behaviors in which many adults freely engage but which I would never call upon government to ban: sky diving and bungee jumping are just two of them. Statistics show that merely attending or teaching in certain inner city government schools is pretty risky too—and maybe more so than occasionally inhaling somebody's smoke.

This is about as slippery a slope as slopes can possibly get slippery. Concede that it's proper for government to dictate what activities a person can engage in when they only involve himself, and where does it stop? Some people read really bad books. Should we take those from them, especially the ones that may champion what some regard as quack remedies or, heaven forbid, those that even propagate resistance to the state? And how about those sugary drinks that former New York City Mayor Michael "Nanny" Bloomberg tried to punish restaurant owners for selling to willing customers? Will progressives please tell us how invasive they ultimately want the state to be for our own good?

It seems to me that enforcing private property rights (in both your body and the physical goods you can rightfully claim as yours) produces a far more precise and predictable set of rules for a civilized society. Rather than a sweeping mandate to coercively adjust our behaviors in ways that somebody in government thinks would be good for us, wouldn't it make more sense to define property rights and then enforce them? Allow for voluntary, peaceful interactions and punish only those actions that do violence to the rights or property of others. You can smoke all you want, as long as you don't blow smoke in my face or smoke next to me in a restaurant that declares "No smoking."

Of course, the more we "socialize" things, the more invasive and intrusive the state must necessarily become. If everybody is paying for everybody else's health care through government redistribution programs, for instance, then everybody has an incentive to scrutinize, denounce and regulate everybody else's behavior. If I'm paying for your food stamps, then I don't want to see you in line in front of me at the grocery store buying junk food with them. But if you're paying for your own groceries, then it's none of my business. This is an argument for peace and minding your own business by *avoiding* the socialization of human affairs, lest we all become nosy, petty dictators.

The statist impulse is a preference for deploying the force of the state to achieve some benefit—real or imagined, for one's self or others—over voluntary alternatives such as persuasion, education or free choice. If people saw the options in such stark terms, or if they realized the slippery slope they're on when they endorse government intervention, support for resolving matters through force would likely diminish. The problem is, they frequently fail to equate intervention with force. But that is precisely what's involved, is it not? The state government in Florida did not *request* that restaurants forbid smoking; it *ordered* them to under threat of fines and imprisonment.

I tried this reasoning on some of my friends. Except for the diehard libertarians, here were some typical attitudes and how they were expressed:

Delusion: "It's not really 'force' if a majority of citizens support it."

Paternalism: "In this instance, force was a positive thing because it was for your own good."

Dependency: "If government won't do it, who will?"

Myopia: "You're making a mountain out of a molehill. How can banning smoking in restaurants possibly be a threat to liberty? If it is, it's so minor that it doesn't matter."

Impatience: "I don't want to wait until my favorite restaurant gets around to banning it on its own."

Power lust: "Restaurants that won't keep smoke out have to be told to do it."

Self-absorption: "I just don't care. I hate smoke and I don't want to chance smelling it even if a restaurant owner puts the smokers in their own section."

On a larger scale, every one of these arguments can be employed—indeed, they are invariably employed—to justify shackling a people with intolerable limitations on their liberties. If there's one thing we must learn from the history of regimes, it is that you give them an inch and sooner or later, by appealing to popular weaknesses, they will take a mile. The challenge is getting people to understand that liberty is more often eaten away one small bite at a time than in one big gulp, and that it's wiser to resist liberty's erosion in small things than it is to concede and hope that bigger battles won't have to be fought later.

Delusion, paternalism, dependency, myopia, impatience, power lust and self-absorption: All are reasons people succumb to the statist impulse. As I pondered this, it occurred to me that they are also vestiges of infantile thinking. As children or adolescents, our understanding of how the world works is half-baked at best. We expect others to provide for us and don't much care how they get what they give us. And we want it now.

We consider ourselves "adults" when we learn there are boundaries beyond which our behavior should not tread; when we think of the long run and all people instead of just ourselves and the here and now; when we make every effort to be as independent as our physical and mental abilities allow; when we leave others alone unless they threaten us; and when we patiently satisfy our desires through peaceful means rather than with a club. We consider ourselves "adults" when we embrace personal responsibility; we revert to infantile behavior when we shun it.

Yet survey the landscape of American public policy debate these days and you find no end to the demands to utilize the force of the state to "do something." Tax the other guy because he has more than me. Give me a tariff so I can be relieved of my foreign competition. Subsidize my college education. Swipe that property so I can put a hotel on it. Fix this or that problem for me, and fix it pronto. Make my life easier by making somebody else pay. Tell that guy who owns a restaurant that he can't serve people who want to smoke.

I wonder if America has become a giant nursery, full of screaming babies who see the state as their loving nanny. It makes me want to say, "Grow up!"

Societies rise or fall depending on how civil its citizens are. The more they respect each other and associate freely, the safer and more prosperous they are. The more they rely on force — legal or not — the more pliant they are in the hands of demagogues and tyrants. So resisting the statist impulse is no trivial issue. In my mind, resisting that impulse is nothing less than the adult thing to do.

(Editor's Note:. The original version of this essay appeared in FEE's magazine, The Freeman, *in October 2006 under the title, "Growing Up Means Resisting the Statist Impulse.")*

SUMMARY

- It's easy to fall into the trap of the "quick fix" that suggests the use of force to address a perceived problem. A thinking person will step back and consider the consequences, *all* of them, including the impact on individual rights
- Private property rights, clearly stated and strictly enforced, provide a better framework for society's rules than the whims of people who want to dictate to others what's good for them
- Delusion, paternalism, dependency, myopia, impatience, power lust and self-absorption may prompt us to call the cops but are hardly sound motivations for government policy

28

"GOVERNMENT SPENDING BRINGS JOBS AND PROSPERITY"

By Henry Hazlitt

A YOUNG HOODLUM HEAVES A BRICK THROUGH THE WINDOW OF A BAKER'S SHOP. The shopkeeper runs out furious, but the boy is gone. A crowd gathers, and begins to stare with quiet dissatisfaction at the gaping hole in the window and the shattered glass all over the bread and pies. After a while the crowd feels the need for philosophic reflection. And several of its members are almost certain to remind each other or the baker that, after all, the misfortune has its bright side. It will make business for some glazier.

As they begin to think of this, they elaborate upon it. How much does a new plate glass window cost? Three hundred dollars? That will be quite a sum. After all, if windows were never broken, what would happen to the glass business? Then, of course, the thing is endless. The glazier will have $300 more to spend with other merchants, and these in turn will have $300 more to spend with still other merchants, and so *ad infinitum*. The smashed window will go on providing money and employment in ever-widening circles. The logical conclusion from all this would be, if the crowd drew it, that the little hoodlum who threw the brick, far from being a public menace, was a public benefactor.

Now let us take another look. The crowd is at least right in its first conclusion. This little act of vandalism will in the first instance mean more business for some glazier. The glazier will be no more unhappy to learn of the incident than an undertaker is to learn of a death. But the shopkeeper will be out $300 that he was planning to spend for a new suit. Because he has had to replace a window, he will have to go without the suit (or some equivalent need or luxury). Instead of having a window and $300 he now has merely a window. Or, as he was planning to buy the suit that very afternoon, instead of having both a window and a suit he must be content with the window and no suit. If we think of him as part of the community, the community has lost a new suit that might otherwise have come into being, and is just that much poorer.

The glazier's gain of business, in short, is merely the tailor's loss of business. No new "employment" has been added. The people in the crowd were thinking only of two parties to the transaction, the baker and the glazier. They had forgotten the potential third party involved, the tailor. They forgot him precisely because he will not now enter the scene. They will see the new window in the next day or two. They will never see the extra suit, precisely because it will never be made. The see only what is immediately visible to the eye.

So we have finished with the broken window, an elementary fallacy. Anybody, one would think, would be able to avoid it after a few moments' thought. Yet the broken-window fallacy, under a hundred disguises, is the most persistent in the history of economics. It is more rampant now than at any time in the past. It is solemnly reaffirmed every day by great captains of industry, by chambers of commerce, by labor union leaders, by editorial writers and newspaper columnists and radio commentators, by learned statisticians using the most refined techniques, by professors of economics in our best universities. In their various ways they all dilate upon the advantages of destruction or they declare that the mere act of government spending "stimulates" without ever asking where the money must come from.

Though some of them would disdain to say that there are net benefits in small acts of destruction, they see almost endless benefits in enormous acts of destruction. *(Editor's Note: "progressive" economists like Paul Krugman see no problem in suggesting the economy would be stimulated if your house is blown up but has so far they have not done their part to goose the economy by blowing up their own.)*

They see "miracles of production" which require a war to achieve. And they see a world made prosperous by an enormous "accumulated" or "pent-up" demand. After World War II in Europe, they joyously counted the houses—the whole cities—that "had to be replaced." In America they counted the houses that could not be built during the war, the nylon stockings that could not be supplied, the worn-out automobiles and tires, the obsolescent radios and refrigerators. They brought together formidable totals.

It was merely our old friend, the broken-window fallacy, in new clothing, and grown fat beyond recognition.

(Editor's Note: Henry Hazlitt's inspiration for this essay was the French economist Frédéric Bastiat. The most notable of Hazlitt's many books was the popular Economics in One Lesson, *from which this essay is adapted, available for no charge on FEE.org.)*

SUMMARY

- The broken-window fallacy essentially calls us to be thorough in our thinking. It's not enough to simply see the immediate or what strikes the eye. We must also consider the long-run effects of an act or policy on all people
- When government "spending" seems to stimulate, it's because we're not seeing its redistributive nature. If government spends more, then there is precisely that much less spending done by those from whom the money is taken. If the government spends more and borrows to pay for it

29

"UPTON SINCLAIR'S *THE JUNGLE* PROVED REGULATION WAS REQUIRED"

By Lawrence W. Reed

A LITTLE OVER A CENTURY AGO, A GREAT AND ENDURING MYTH WAS BORN. MUCK-
raking novelist Upton Sinclair wrote a novel entitled *The Jungle*—a tale
of greed and abuse that still reverberates as a case against a free economy.
Sinclair's "jungle" was unregulated enterprise; his example was the meat-
packing industry; his purpose was government regulation. The culmina-
tion of his work was the passage in 1906 of the Meat Inspection Act,
enshrined in history, or at least in history books, as a sacred cow (excuse
the pun) of the interventionist state.

A century later, American schoolchildren are still being taught a
simplistic and romanticized version of this history. For many young
people, *The Jungle* is required reading in high-school classes, where they
are led to believe that unscrupulous capitalists were routinely tainting
our meat, and that moral crusader Upton Sinclair rallied the public and
forced government to shift from pusillanimous bystander to heroic do-
gooder, valiantly disciplining the marketplace to protect its millions of
victims.

But this is a triumph of myth over reality, of ulterior motives over good intentions. Reading *The Jungle* and assuming it's a credible news source is like watching *Star Wars* because you think it's a documentary.

Given the book's favorable publicity, it's not surprising that it has duped a lot of people. Ironically, Sinclair himself, as a founder of the Intercollegiate Socialist Society in 1905, was personally suckered by more than a few intellectual charlatans of his day. One of them was fellow "investigative journalist" Lincoln Steffens, best known for returning from the Soviet Union in 1921 and saying, "I have seen the future, and it works."

In any event, there is much about *The Jungle* that Americans just don't learn from conventional history texts.

The Jungle was, first and foremost, a novel. As is indicated by the fact that the book originally appeared as a serialization in the socialist journal "Appeal to Reason," it was intended to be a polemic—a diatribe, if you will—not a well-researched and dispassionate documentary. Sinclair relied heavily both on his own imagination and on the hearsay of others. He did not even pretend that he had actually witnessed the horrendous conditions he ascribed to Chicago packinghouses, nor to have verified them, nor to have derived them from any official records.

Sinclair hoped the book would ignite a powerful socialist movement on behalf of America's workers. The public's attention focused instead on his fewer than a dozen pages of supposed descriptions of unsanitary conditions in the meat-packing plants. "I aimed at the public's heart," he later wrote, "and by accident I hit it in the stomach."

Though his novelized and sensational accusations prompted congressional investigations of the industry, the investigators themselves expressed skepticism about Sinclair's integrity and credibility as a source of information. In July 1906, President Theodore Roosevelt stated his opinion of Sinclair in a letter to journalist William Allen White: "I have an utter contempt for him. He is hysterical, unbalanced, and untruthful. Three-fourths of the things he said were absolute falsehoods. For some of the remainder there was only a basis of truth."

Sinclair's fellow writer and philosophical intimate, Jack London, wrote this announcement of *The Jungle*, a promo that was approved by Sinclair himself:

> Dear Comrades:...The book we have been waiting for these many years! It will open countless ears that have been deaf to Socialism. It will make thousands of converts to our cause. It depicts what our country really is, the home of oppression and injustice, a nightmare of misery, an inferno of suffering, a human hell, a jungle of wild beasts.
>
> And take notice and remember, comrades, this book is straight proletarian. It is written by an intellectual proletarian, for the proletarian. It is to be published by a proletarian publishing house. It is to be read by the proletariat. What "Uncle Tom's Cabin" did for the black slaves "The Jungle" has a large chance to do for the white slaves of today.

The fictitious characters of Sinclair's novel tell of men falling into tanks in meat-packing plants and being ground up with animal parts, then made into "Durham's Pure Leaf Lard." Historian Stewart H. Holbrook writes, "The grunts, the groans, the agonized squeals of animals being butchered, the rivers of blood, the steaming masses of intestines, the various stenches...were displayed along with the corruption of government inspectors" and, of course, the callous greed of the ruthless packers.

Most Americans would be surprised to know that government meat inspection did not begin in 1906. The inspectors Holbrook cites as being mentioned in Sinclair's book were among hundreds employed by federal, state, and local governments for more than a decade. Indeed, Congressman E. D. Crumpacker of Indiana noted in testimony before the House Agriculture Committee in June 1906 that not even one of those officials "ever registered any complaint or [gave] any public information with respect to the manner of the slaughtering or preparation of meat or food products."

To Crumpacker and other contemporary skeptics, "Either the Government officials in Chicago [were] woefully derelict in their duty, or the situation over there [had been] outrageously overstated to the country." If the packing plants were as bad as alleged in *The Jungle*, surely the government inspectors who never said so must be judged as guilty of neglect as the packers were of abuse.

Some two million visitors came to tour the stockyards and packinghouses of Chicago every year. Thousands of people worked in both. Why did it take a novel, written by an anti-capitalist ideologue who spent but a few weeks in the city, to unveil the real conditions to the American public? And why, to this day, do we not know the name of the men who supposedly fell into tanks and became "Durham's Pure Leaf Lard"? Didn't one of their co-workers, friends or relatives ever come forward and ask, "Hey, what happened to Bob?"

All the big Chicago packers combined accounted for less than 50 percent of the meat products produced in the United States, but few if any charges were ever made against the sanitary conditions of the packinghouses of other cities. If the Chicago packers were guilty of anything like the terribly unsanitary conditions suggested by Sinclair, wouldn't they be foolishly exposing themselves to devastating losses of market share?

In this connection, historians with an ideological axe to grind against the market usually ignore an authoritative 1906 report of the Department of Agriculture's Bureau of Animal Husbandry. Its investigators provided a point-by-point refutation of the worst of Sinclair's allegations, some of which they labeled as "willful and deliberate misrepresentations of fact," "atrocious exaggeration," and "not at all characteristic."

Instead, some of these same historians dwell on the Neill-Reynolds Report of the same year because it at least tentatively supported Sinclair. It turns out that neither Neill nor Reynolds had any experience in the meat-packing business and spent a grand total of two and a half weeks in the spring of 1906 investigating and preparing what turned out to be a carelessly written report with predetermined conclusions. Gabriel Kolko, a socialist but nonetheless a historian with a respect for facts, dismisses Sinclair as a propagandist and assails Neill and Reynolds as "two inexperienced Washington bureaucrats who freely admitted they knew nothing" of the meat-packing process. Their own subsequent testimony revealed that they had gone to Chicago with the intention of finding fault with industry practices so as to get a new inspection law passed.

According to the popular myth, there were no government inspectors before Congress acted in response to *The Jungle*, and the greedy meat packers fought federal inspection all the way. The truth is that not only did government inspection exist, but meat packers themselves supported it and were in the forefront of the effort to extend it so as to ensnare their smaller, unregulated competitors.

When the sensational accusations of *The Jungle* became worldwide news, foreign purchases of American meat were cut in half and the meat packers looked for new regulations to give their markets a calming sense of security. The only congressional hearings on what ultimately became the Meat Inspection Act of 1906 were held by Congressman James Wadsworth's Agriculture Committee between June 6 and 11. A careful reading of the deliberations of the Wadsworth committee and the subsequent floor debate leads inexorably to one conclusion: knowing that a new law would allay public fears fanned by *The Jungle*, bring smaller rivals under controls, and put a newly laundered government seal of approval on their products, the major meat packers strongly endorsed the proposed act and only quibbled over who should pay for it.

In the end, Americans got a new federal meat inspection law, the big packers got the taxpayers to pick up the entire $3 million price tag for its implementation, as well as new regulations on the competition, and another myth entered the annals of anti-market dogma.

To his credit, Sinclair actually opposed the law because he saw it for what it really was—a boon for the big meat packers. He had been a fool and a sucker who ended up being used by the very industry he hated. But then, there may not have been an industry that he didn't hate.

Sinclair published more than 90 books before he died (at the age of 90) in 1968—*King Coal, Oil!, The Profits of Religion, The Flivver King,*

Money Writes!, *The Moneychangers*, *The Goose-Step: A Study of American Education*, *The Goslings: A Study of the American Schools*, et cetera—but none came anywhere close to the fame of *The Jungle*. One (*Dragon's Teeth*), about the Nazi rise to power, earned him a Pulitzer in 1942, but almost all the others were little-noticed and even poorly written class warfare screeds and shabby "exposés" of one industry or another. Many were commercial flops. Friend and fellow writer Sinclair Lewis took Sinclair to task for his numerous errors in a letter written to him in January 1928:

> I did not want to say these unpleasant things, but you have written to me, asking my opinion, and I give it to you, flat. If you would get over two ideas—first that anyone who criticizes you is an evil and capitalist-controlled spy, and second that you have only to spend a few weeks on any subject to become a master of it—you might yet regain your now totally lost position as the leader of American socialistic journalism.

On three occasions, Sinclair's radical socialism led him into electoral politics. Running on the Socialist Party ticket for a congressional seat in New Jersey in 1906, he captured a measly three percent of the vote. He didn't fare much better as the Socialist candidate for governor of California in 1926. In 1934, however, he secured the nomination of the Democratic Party for the California governorship and shook up the political establishment with a program he called EPIC ("End Poverty in California"). With unemployment in excess of 20 percent and the state seething in discontent, most Californians still couldn't stomach Sinclair's penchant for goofy boondoggles and snake oil promises. Nonetheless, he garnered a very respectable 38 percent against the incumbent Republican Frank Merriman.

The EPIC platform is worth a mention, if only to underscore Sinclair's lifelong, unshakeable fascination with crackpot central-planning contrivances. It called for a massive tax increase on corporations and utilities, huge public employment programs (he wanted to put the unemployed to work on farms seized by the state for failure to pay taxes), and the issuance of money-like "scrip" based on goods produced by state-employed workers. He thought the Depression was probably a permanent affliction of capitalism and seemed utterly unaware of the endless state interventions that had brought it on in the first place (see my "Great Myths of the Great Depression" at FEE.org).

Was Upton Sinclair a nincompoop? You decide. This much is clear: early in the 20th century, he cooked up a work of fiction as a device to help in his agitation for an economic system (socialism) that doesn't work and that was already known not to work. For the next six decades he learned little if anything about economics, but he never relented in his support for discredited schemes to put big government in charge of other people's lives.

Myths survive their makers. What you've just read about Sinclair and his myth is not at all "politically correct." But defending the market from historical attack begins with explaining what really happened in our history. Those who persist in the shallow claim that *The Jungle* stands as a compelling indictment of the market should take a look at the history surrounding this honored novel. Upon inspection, there seems to be an unpleasant odor hovering over it.

(Editor's Note: Versions of this essay have appeared in print in several places since 1994, notably in FEE's magazine, The Freeman, *and* Liberty *magazine.)*

SUMMARY

- Upton Sinclair's novel, *The Jungle,* is treated by progressives as though it were a documentary, but it was nothing of the kind. It was a work of fiction, full of fabrications. Even Teddy Roosevelt said the author was "hysterical and untruthful." Sinclair was hired to write it for the purpose of advancing socialism in America
- Government meat inspection existed before Sinclair's book was ever written. If even a portion of what he wrote really

30

"CAPITALISM'S INDUSTRIAL REVOLUTION CURSED THE WORLD WITH THE HORROR OF CHILD LABOR"

By Lawrence W. Reed

PROFOUND ECONOMIC CHANGES TOOK PLACE IN GREAT BRITAIN IN THE CENTURY after 1750. This was the age of the Industrial Revolution, complete with a cascade of technical innovations, a vast increase in production, a renaissance of world trade, and rapid growth of urban populations.

Where historians and other observers clash is in the interpretation of these great changes. Did they represent improvement to the citizens or did these events set them back? Perhaps no other issue within this realm has generated more intellectual heat than the one concerning the labor of children. Critics of capitalism have successfully cast this matter as an irrefutable indictment of the capitalist system as it was emerging in nineteenth-century Britain.

The many reports of poor working conditions and long hours of difficult toil make harrowing reading, to be sure. William Cooke Taylor wrote at the time about contemporary reformers who, witnessing children at work in factories, thought to themselves, "How much more delightful would have been the gambol of the free limbs on the hillside; the sight of the green mead with its spangles of buttercups and daisies; the song of the bird and the humming of the bee." But as any honest historian will tell you, most children before the Industrial Revolution did not survive past the age of five; those who did went to work at an early age because productivity was so low that most parents couldn't afford the children to be idle. In pre-capitalist, feudal times, passing a law to prevent children from working would have meant mass starvation.

Of those historians who have interpreted child labor in industrial Britain as a crime of capitalism, none have been more prominent than J. L. and Barbara Hammond. Their many works have been widely promoted as "authoritative" on the issue.

The Hammonds divided the factory children into two classes: "parish apprentice children" and "free labour children." It is a distinction of enormous significance, though one the authors themselves failed utterly to appreciate. Having made the distinction, the Hammonds proceeded to treat the two classes as though no distinction between them existed at all. A deluge of false and misleading conclusions about capitalism and child labor has poured forth for years as a consequence.

"Free labour" children were those who lived at home but worked during the day in factories at the insistence of their parents or guardians. British historian E. P. Thompson, though generally critical of the factory system, nonetheless quite properly conceded that "it is perfectly true that the parents not only needed their children's earnings, but expected them to work."

Ludwig von Mises, the great Austrian economist, put it well when he noted that the generally deplorable conditions extant for centuries before the Industrial Revolution, and the low levels of productivity that created them, caused families to embrace the new opportunities the factories represented: "It is a distortion of facts to say that the factories carried off the housewives from the nurseries and the kitchen and the children from their play. These women had nothing to cook with and to feed their children. These children were destitute and starving. Their

Though it is inaccurate to judge capitalism guilty of the sins of parish apprenticeship, it would also be inaccurate to assume that free labor children worked under ideal conditions in the early days of the Industrial Revolution. By today's standards their situation was clearly bad. Such capitalist achievements as air conditioning and high levels of productivity would in time substantially ameliorate working conditions, however. The evidence in favor of capitalism is thus compellingly suggestive: From 1750 to 1850, when the population of Great Britain nearly tripled, the virtually exclusive choice of those flocking to the country for jobs was to work for private capitalists.

Conditions of employment and sanitation were best, as the Factory Commission of 1833 documented, in the larger and newer factories. The owners of these larger establishments, which were more easily and frequently subject to visitation and scrutiny by inspectors, increasingly chose to dismiss children from employment rather than be subjected to elaborate, arbitrary, and ever-changing rules on how they might run a factory employing youths. The result of legislative intervention was that these dismissed children, most of whom needed to work in order to survive, were forced to seek jobs in smaller, older, and more out-of-the-way places where sanitation, lighting, and safety were markedly inferior. Those who could not find new jobs were reduced to the status of their counterparts a hundred years before—that is, to irregular and grueling agricultural labor or, in the words of Mises, "to infest the country as vagabonds, beggars, tramps, robbers, and prostitutes."

Child labor was relieved of its worst attributes not by legislative fiat but by the progressive march of an ever more productive capitalist system. Child labor was virtually eliminated when, for the first time in history, the productivity of parents in free labor markets rose to the point where it was no longer economically necessary for children to work to survive. The emancipators and benefactors of children were n legislators or factory inspectors but factory owners and financiers. T' efforts and investments in machinery led to a rise in real wages only refuge was the factory. It saved them, in the strict sense of the term, from death by starvation."

Private factory owners could not forcibly subjugate "free labour" children; they could not compel them to work in conditions their parents found unacceptable. The mass exodus from the continent to increasingly capitalist, industrial Britain in the first half of the nineteenth century strongly suggests that people did indeed find the industrial order an attractive alternative. And there's no credible evidence suggesting that parents in these early capitalist days were any less caring of their off-spring than those of pre-capitalist times.

The situation, however, was much different for "parish apprentice" children. Close examination reveals that the critics were focusing on these children when they spoke of the "evils" of capitalism's Industrial Revolution. These youngsters, it turns out, were under the direct author-ity and supervision not of their parents in a free labor market, but of government officials. Most were orphans; a few were victims of negligent parents or parents whose health or lack of skills kept them from earning sufficient income to care for a family. All were in the custody of "parish authorities." As the Hammonds themselves wrote, "[T]he first mills were placed on streams, and the necessary labour was provided by the impor-tation of cartloads of pauper children from the workhouses of the big towns.... To the parish authorities, encumbered with great masses of unwanted children, the new cotton mills in Lancashire, Derby, and Notts were a godsend."

Though consigned to the control of a government authority, these children are routinely held up as victims of capitalist greed. But as histo-rian Robert Hessen writes, those very children "were sent into virtual slavery by a government body; they were deserted or orphaned pauper children who were legally under the custody of the poor-law officials in the parish, and who were bound by these officials into long terms of unpaid apprenticeship in return for bare subsistence." Indeed, the first act in Britain that applied to factory children was passed to protect these very parish apprentices, not "free labour" children.

growing abundance of goods at lower prices, and to an incomparable improvement in the general standard of living.

(Editor's Note: This essay is condensed from one the author first published in 1976, entitled "Child Labor and the British Industrial Revolution," available at Mackinac.org.

SUMMARY

- Children worked before the Industrial Revolution. It was the Industrial Revolution, in fact, which improved productivity so that eventually parents could earn enough to afford to leave their children at home
- In Britain, the distinction between "free labour" children and "parish apprentice" children must be understood. The latter were under the care of often indifferent government officials, and the result can hardly be laid at the exclusive doorstep of capitalism

31

"LABOR UNIONS RAISE WAGES AND THE STANDARD OF LIVING"

By Hans F. Sennholz

TO BELIEVE THAT LABOR UNIONS ACTUALLY IMPROVE THE LOT OF WORKING PEOPLE is to suggest that the capitalist economy fails to provide fair wages and decent working conditions. It is to imply that a free economy does not work satisfactorily unless it is "fortified" by union activity and government intervention.

The truth is that the unhampered market society allocates to every member the undiminished fruits of his labor. It does so in all ages and societies where individual freedom and private property are safeguarded. *(Editor's Note: The process works faster and more efficiently in our high-tech, information age with a labor force more mobile than ever before but it worked in previous times too, so long as individuals were free to accept or reject the offers of employers, or to leave one employer and work either for another or for himself.)*

The reason your great-grandfather earned $5 a week for 60 hours of labor must be sought in his low productivity, not in the absence of labor unions. The $5 he earned constituted full and fair payment for his productive efforts—a voluntary contract he likely entered into because it represented his best opportunity. The economic principles of the free market, the competition among employers, a man's mobility and freedom of choice, assured him full wages under the given production conditions.

Wages were low and working conditions primitive because labor productivity was low, machines and tools were relatively primitive, technology and production methods were crude when compared with today's. If, for any reason, our productivity were to sink back to that of our forebears, *our* wages, too, would decline to their levels and our work week would lengthen again no matter what the activities of labor unions or the decrees of government.

In a free market economy, labor productivity determines wage rates. As it is the undeniable policy of labor unions to reduce this productivity (as measured per man-hour) by forcing compensation up or spreading out the work with restrictive work rules, they have in fact reduced the wages of the masses of people although some privileged members have benefited temporarily at the expense of others. This is true especially today when the unions enjoy many legal immunities and considerable political powers. And it also was true during the nineteenth century when our ancestors labored from dawn to dusk for low wages.

Through a variety of coercive measures, labor unions merely impose higher labor costs on employers. The higher costs reduce the returns on capital and curtail production, which curbs the opportunities for employment. This is why our centers of unionism are also our centers of highest unemployment; they are also the industries that have seen the most dramatic declines in numbers of existing jobs, because like anything else, the higher the price, the less will be purchased. *(Editor's Note: It's also why compulsory unionism states for years have shown lower rates of both employment growth and wage rates than so-called "right-to-work" states.)*

True enough, the senior union members who happen to keep their jobs do enjoy higher wages. But those who can no longer find jobs in unionized industries then seek employment in nonunionized activity. This influx and absorption of excess labor tends to reduce *their* wages.

The resulting difference between union and nonunion wages rates gives rise to the notion that labor unions must indeed benefit workers. In reality, the presence of the nonunionized sectors of the labor market hides the disastrous consequences of union policy by preventing mass unemployment. *(Editor's Note: Nonetheless, with 94 percent of today's private sector workers being completely non-union, and many of them enjoying very high wage rates, it's increasingly difficult for unions to argue that workers without unions are exploited and unprotected.)*

(Editor's Note: This essay, with minor updates, was first published in the 1962 book, Clichés of Socialism.*)*

SUMMARY

- Wages can only be paid out of what is produced (no production, no wages), therefore greater productivity is the key to higher wages
- Unions typically hamper production. Union activity may result in some people getting more but without an increase in productivity, that simply means that some other people must get less. Either you bake a bigger pie for everybody or you just slice the pie up differently
- It looks sometimes like unions have actually forced wages higher because of the lower wages in non-unionized businesses. But the latter are caused in part by the outflow of labor from unionized sectors to non-unionized ones. Unionized auto-workers today, for example, may make a little more per hour than their nonunionized counterparts but there are a lot fewer of them too!

32

"FDR WAS ELECTED IN 1932 ON A PROGRESSIVE PLATFORM TO PLAN THE ECONOMY"

By Lawrence W. Reed

HARRY TRUMAN ONCE SAID, "THE ONLY THING NEW IN THE WORLD IS THE HISTORY you don't know." That observation applies especially well to what tens of millions of Americans have been taught about Franklin Delano Roosevelt, the man under whom Truman served as vice president for about a month.

Recent scholarship (including a highly acclaimed book, *New Deal or Raw Deal*, by Young America's Foundation's speaker and a FEE senior historian Burton Folsom) is thankfully disabusing Americans of the once-popular myth that FDR saved us from the Great Depression.

Another example is a 2004 article by two UCLA economists—Harold L. Cole and Lee E. Ohanian—in the important mainstream *Journal of Political Economy*. They observed that Franklin Roosevelt extended the Great Depression by seven long years. "The economy was poised for a beautiful recovery," the authors show, "but that recovery was stalled by these misguided policies."

In a commentary on Cole and Ohanian's research ("The New Deal Debunked (again)," available on Mises.org), Loyola University economist Thomas DiLorenzo pointed out that six years after FDR took office, unemployment was almost six times the pre-Depression level. Per capita GDP, personal consumption expenditures, and net private investment were all lower in 1939 than they were in 1929.

"The fact that it has taken 'mainstream' neoclassical economists so long to recognize [that FDR's policies exacerbated the disaster]," notes DiLorenzo, "is truly astounding," but still "better late than never."

A considerable degree of central planning in Washington is certainly what Franklin Roosevelt delivered, but it was not what he promised when he was first elected in 1932. My own essay on this period, "Great Myths of the Great Depression" found on FEE.org) provides many details, based on the very platform and promises on which FDR ran. But until recently, I was unaware of a long-forgotten book that makes the case as well as any.

Hell Bent for Election was written by James P. Warburg, a banker who witnessed the 1932 election and the first two years of Roosevelt's first term from the inside. Warburg, the son of prominent financier and Federal Reserve cofounder Paul Warburg, was no less than a high-level financial adviser to FDR himself. Disillusioned with the President, he left the administration in 1934 and wrote his book a year later.

Warburg voted for the man who said this on March 2, 1930, as Governor of New York:

> The doctrine of regulation and legislation by "master minds,"
> in whose judgment and will all the people may gladly and
> quietly acquiesce, has been too glaringly apparent at Wash-
> ington during these last ten years. Were it possible to find
> "master minds" so unselfish, so willing to decide unhesitat-
> ingly against their own personal interests or private preju-
> dices, men almost godlike in their ability to hold the scales
> of justice with an even hand, such a government might be to
> the interests of the country; but there are none such on our

political horizon, and we cannot expect a complete reversal of all the teachings of history.

What Warburg and the country actually elected in 1932 was a man whose subsequent performance looks little like the platform and promises on which he ran and a lot like those of that year's Socialist Party candidate, Norman Thomas.

Who campaigned for a "drastic" reduction of 25 percent in federal spending, a balanced federal budget, a rollback of government intrusion into agriculture, and restoration of a sound gold currency? Roosevelt did. Who called the administration of incumbent Herbert Hoover "the greatest spending administration in peace time in all our history" and assailed it for raising taxes and tariffs? Roosevelt did. FDR's running mate, John Nance Garner, even declared that Hoover "was leading the country down the road to socialism."

It was socialist Norman Thomas, not Franklin Roosevelt, who proposed massive increases in federal spending and deficits and sweeping interventions into the private economy—and he barely mustered 2 percent of the vote. When the dust settled, Warburg shows, we got what Thomas promised, more of what Hoover had been lambasted for, and almost nothing that FDR himself had pledged. FDR employed more "master minds" to plan the economy than perhaps all previous presidents combined.

After detailing the promises and the duplicity, Warburg offered this assessment of the man who betrayed him and the country:

> Much as I dislike to say so, it is my honest conviction that Mr. Roosevelt has utterly lost his sense of proportion. He sees himself as the one man who can save the country, as the one man who can "save capitalism from itself," as the one man who knows what is good for us and what is not. He sees himself as indispensable. And when a man thinks of himself as being indispensable...that man is headed for trouble.

Was FDR an economic wizard? Warburg reveals nothing of the sort, observing that FDR was "undeniably and shockingly superficial about anything that relates to finance." He was driven not by logic, facts, or humility but by "his emotional desires, predilections, and prejudices."

"Mr. Roosevelt," wrote Warburg, "gives me the impression that he can really believe what he wants to believe, really think what he wants to think, and really remember what he wants to remember, to a greater extent than anyone I have ever known." Less charitable observers might diagnose the problem as "delusions of grandeur."

"I believe that Mr. Roosevelt is so charmed with the fun of brandishing the band leader's baton at the head of the parade, so pleased with the picture he sees of himself, that he is no longer capable of recognizing that the human power to lead is limited, that the 'new ideas' of leadership dished up to him by his bright young men in the Brain Trust are nothing but old ideas that have been tried before, and that one cannot uphold the social order defined in the Constitution and at the same time undermine it," Warburg lamented.

So if Warburg was right (and I believe he was), Franklin Delano Roosevelt misled the country with his promises in 1932 and put personal ambition and power lust in charge—not a very uncommon thing as politicians go. In any event, the country got a nice little bait-and-switch deal, and the economy languished as a result.

In the world of economics and free exchange, the rule is that you get what you pay for. The 1932 election is perhaps the best example of the rule that prevails all too often in the political world: You get what you voted against.

SUMMARY

- Franklin Roosevelt delivered a lot of central planning from Washington but that wasn't what he asked voters to endorse in the 1932 election

- FDR attacked Hoover for greatly increasing taxes and spending but once elected, did even more of both
- FDR's close adviser, James Warburg, thought that FDR was economically illiterate and politically opportunistic

33

"THE GREAT DEPRESSION WAS A CALAMITY OF UNFETTERED CAPITALISM"

By Lawrence W. Reed

HOW BAD WAS THE GREAT DEPRESSION? OVER THE FOUR YEARS FROM 1929 TO 1933, production at the nation's factories, mines, and utilities fell by more than half. People's real disposable incomes dropped 28 percent. Stock prices collapsed to one-tenth of their pre-crash height. The number of unemployed Americans rose from 1.6 million in 1929 to 12.8 million in 1933. One of every four workers was out of a job at the Depression's nadir, and ugly rumors of revolt simmered for the first time since the Civil War.

Old myths never die; they just keep showing up in college economics and political science textbooks. Students today are frequently taught that unfettered free enterprise collapsed of its own weight in 1929, paving the way for a decade-long economic depression full of hardship and misery. President Herbert Hoover is presented as an advocate of "hands-off," or laissez-faire, economic policy, while his successor, Franklin Roosevelt, is the economic savior whose policies brought us recovery. This popular account of the Depression belongs in a book of fairy tales and not in a serious discussion of economic history, as a review of the facts demonstrates.

To properly understand the events of the time, it is appropriate to view the Great Depression as not one, but four consecutive depressions rolled into one. The late economist Hans F. Sennholz labeled these four "phases" as follows: the business cycle; the disintegration of the world economy; the New Deal; and the Wagner Act. The first phase explains why the crash of 1929 happened in the first place; the other three show how government intervention kept the economy in a stupor for over a decade.

The Great Depression was not the country's first depression, though it proved to be the longest. The common thread woven through the several earlier debacles was disastrous manipulation of the money supply by government. For various reasons, government policies were adopted that ballooned the quantity of money and credit. A boom resulted, followed later by a painful day of reckoning. None of America's depressions prior to 1929, however, lasted more than four years and most of them were over in two. The Great Depression lasted for a dozen years because the government compounded its monetary errors with a series of harmful interventions.

Most monetary economists, particularly those of the "Austrian school," have observed the close relationship between money supply and economic activity. When government inflates the money and credit supply, interest rates at first fall. Businesses invest this "easy money" in new production projects and a boom takes place in capital goods. As the boom matures, business costs rise, interest rates readjust upward, and profits are squeezed. The easy-money effects thus wear off and the monetary authorities, fearing price inflation, slow the growth of or even contract the money supply. In either case, the manipulation is enough to knock out the shaky supports from underneath the economic house of cards.

One of the most thorough and meticulously documented accounts of the Fed's inflationary actions prior to 1929 is *America's Great Depression* by the late Murray Rothbard. Using a broad measure that includes currency, demand and time deposits, and other ingredients, Rothbard estimated that the Federal Reserve expanded the money supply by more than 60 percent from mid-1921 to mid-1929. The flood of easy money drove interest rates down, pushed the stock market to dizzy heights, and gave birth to the "Roaring Twenties." Some economists miss this because they look at measures of the "price level," which didn't change much. But easy money distorts *relative* prices, which in turn fosters unsustainable conditions in certain sectors.

By early 1929, the Federal Reserve was taking the punch away from the party. It choked off the money supply, raised interest rates, and for the next three years presided over a money supply that shrank by 30 percent. This deflation following the inflation wrenched the economy from tremendous boom to colossal bust.

The "smart" money—the Bernard Baruchs and the Joseph Kennedys who watched things like money supply—saw that the party was coming to an end before most other Americans did. Baruch actually began selling stocks and buying bonds and gold as early as 1928; Kennedy did likewise, commenting, "only a fool holds out for the top dollar."

When the masses of investors eventually sensed the change in Fed policy, the stampede was underway. The stock market, after nearly two months of moderate decline, plunged on "Black Thursday"—October 24, 1929—as the pessimistic view of large and knowledgeable investors spread.

The stock market crash was only a symptom—not the cause—of the Great Depression: the market rose and fell in near synchronization with what the Fed was doing. If this crash had been like previous ones, the subsequent hard times might have ended in a year or two. But unprecedented political bungling instead prolonged the misery for twelve long years.

Unemployment in 1930 averaged a mildly recessionary 8.9 percent, up from 3.2 percent in 1929. It shot up rapidly until peaking out at more than 25 percent in 1933. Until March 1933, these were the years of President Herbert Hoover—the man that anti-capitalists depict as a champion of noninterventionist, laissez-faire economics.

Did Hoover really subscribe to a "hands off the economy," free-market philosophy? His opponent in the 1932 election, Franklin Roosevelt, didn't think so. During the campaign, Roosevelt blasted Hoover for spending and taxing too much, boosting the national debt, choking off trade, and putting millions of people on the dole. He accused the president of "reckless and extravagant" spending, of thinking "that we ought to center control of everything in Washington as rapidly as possible," and of presiding over "the greatest spending administration in peacetime in all of history." Roosevelt's running mate, John Nance Garner, charged that Hoover was "leading the country down the path of socialism." Contrary to the modern myth about Hoover, Roosevelt and Garner were absolutely right.

The crowning folly of the Hoover administration was the Smoot-Hawley Tariff, passed in June 1930. It came on top of the Fordney-McCumber Tariff of 1922, which had already put American agriculture in a tailspin during the preceding decade. The most protectionist legislation in U.S. history, Smoot-Hawley virtually closed the borders to foreign goods and ignited a vicious international trade war.

Officials in the administration and in Congress believed that raising trade barriers would force Americans to buy more goods made at home, which would solve the nagging unemployment problem. They ignored an important principle of international commerce: trade is ultimately a two-way street; if foreigners cannot sell their goods here, then they cannot earn the dollars they need to buy here.

Foreign companies and their workers were flattened by Smoot-Hawley's steep tariff rates, and foreign governments soon retaliated with trade barriers of their own. With their ability to sell in the American market severely hampered, they curtailed their purchases of American goods. American agriculture was particularly hard hit. With a stroke of the presidential pen, farmers in this country lost nearly a third of their markets. Farm prices plummeted and tens of thousands of farmers went bankrupt. With the collapse of agriculture, rural banks failed in record numbers, dragging down hundreds of thousands of their customers.

Hoover dramatically increased government spending for subsidy and relief schemes. In the space of one year alone, from 1930 to 1931, the federal government's share of GNP increased by about one-third.

Hoover's agricultural bureaucracy doled out hundreds of millions of dollars to wheat and cotton farmers even as the new tariffs wiped out their markets. His Reconstruction Finance Corporation ladled out billions more in business subsidies. Commenting decades later on Hoover's administration, Rexford Guy Tugwell, one of the architects of Franklin Roosevelt's policies of the 1930s, explained, "We didn't admit it at the time, but practically the whole New Deal was extrapolated from programs that Hoover started."

To compound the folly of high tariffs and huge subsidies, Congress then passed and Hoover signed the Revenue Act of 1932. It doubled the income tax for most Americans; the top bracket more than doubled, going from 24 percent to 63 percent. Exemptions were lowered; the earned income credit was abolished; corporate and estate taxes were raised; new gift, gasoline, and auto taxes were imposed; and postal rates were sharply hiked.

Can any serious scholar observe the Hoover administration's massive economic intervention and, with a straight face, pronounce the inevitably deleterious effects as the fault of free markets?

Franklin Delano Roosevelt won the 1932 presidential election in a landslide, collecting 472 electoral votes to just 59 for the incumbent Herbert Hoover. The platform of the Democratic Party whose ticket Roosevelt headed declared, "We believe that a party platform is a covenant with the people to be faithfully kept by the party entrusted with power." It called for a 25 percent reduction in federal spending, a balanced federal budget, a sound gold currency "to be preserved at all hazards," the removal of government from areas that belonged more appropriately to private enterprise, and an end to the "extravagance" of Hoover's farm programs. This is what candidate Roosevelt promised, but it bears no resemblance to what President Roosevelt actually delivered.

In the first year of the New Deal, Roosevelt proposed spending $10 billion while revenues were only $3 billion. Between 1933 and 1936, government expenditures rose by more than 83 percent. Federal debt skyrocketed by 73 percent.

Roosevelt secured passage of the Agricultural Adjustment Act (AAA), which levied a new tax on agricultural processors and used the revenue to supervise the wholesale destruction of valuable crops and cattle. Federal agents oversaw the ugly spectacle of perfectly good fields of cotton, wheat, and corn being plowed under. Healthy cattle, sheep, and pigs by the millions were slaughtered and buried in mass graves.

Even if the AAA had helped farmers by curtailing supplies and raising prices, it could have done so only by hurting millions of others who had to pay those prices or make do with less to eat.

Perhaps the most radical aspect of the New Deal was the National Industrial Recovery Act (NIRA), passed in June 1933, which set up the National Recovery Administration (NRA). Under the NIRA, most manufacturing industries were suddenly forced into government-mandated cartels. Codes that regulated prices and terms of sale briefly transformed much of the American economy into a fascist-style arrangement, while the NRA was financed by new taxes on the very industries it controlled. Some economists have estimated that the NRA boosted the cost of doing business by an average of 40 percent—not something a depressed economy needed for recovery.

Like Hoover before him, Roosevelt signed into law steep income tax rate increases for the high brackets and introduced a 5 percent withholding tax on corporate dividends. In fact, tax hikes became a favorite policy of the president's for the next ten years, culminating in a top income tax rate of 94 percent during the last year of World War II.

Roosevelt's public relief programs hired actors to give free shows and librarians to catalogue archives. The New Deal even paid researchers to study the history of the safety pin, hired 100 Washington workers to patrol the streets with balloons to frighten starlings away from public buildings, and put men on the public payroll to chase tumbleweeds on windy days.

Roosevelt created the Civil Works Administration in November 1933 and ended it in March 1934, though the unfinished projects were transferred to the Federal Emergency Relief Administration. Roosevelt had assured Congress in his State of the Union message that any new such program would be abolished within a year. "The federal government," said the President, "must and shall quit this business of relief. I am not willing that the vitality of our people be further stopped by the giving of cash, of market baskets, of a few bits of weekly work cutting grass, raking leaves, or picking up papers in the public parks."

But in 1935 the Works Progress Administration came along. It is known today as the very government program that gave rise to the new term, "boondoggle," because it "produced" a lot more than the 77,000 bridges and 116,000 buildings to which its advocates loved to point as evidence of its efficacy. The stupefying roster of wasteful spending generated by these jobs programs represented a diversion of valuable resources to politically motivated and economically counterproductive purposes.

The American economy was soon relieved of the burden of some of the New Deal's excesses when the Supreme Court outlawed the NRA in 1935 and the AAA in 1936, earning Roosevelt's eternal wrath and derision. Recognizing much of what Roosevelt did as unconstitutional, the "nine old men" of the Court also threw out other, more minor acts and programs which hindered recovery. Freed from the worst of the New Deal, the economy showed some signs of life. Unemployment dropped to 18 percent in 1935, 14 percent in 1936, and even lower in 1937. But by 1938, it was back up to 20 percent as the economy slumped again. The stock market crashed nearly 50 percent between August 1937 and March 1938. The "economic stimulus" of Franklin Roosevelt's New Deal had achieved a real "first": a depression within a depression!

The stage was set for the 1937–38 collapse with the passage of the National Labor Relations Act in 1935—better known as the Wagner Act and organized labor's "Magna Carta." To quote Hans Sennholz again:

> This law revolutionized American labor relations. It took
> labor disputes out of the courts of law and brought them

under a newly created Federal agency, the National Labor
Relations Board, which became prosecutor, judge, and jury,
all in one. Labor union sympathizers on the Board further
perverted this law, which already afforded legal immunities
and privileges to labor unions. The U.S. thereby abandoned
a great achievement of Western civilization, equality under
the law.

Armed with these sweeping new powers, labor unions went on a
militant organizing frenzy. Threats, boycotts, strikes, seizures of plants,
and widespread violence pushed productivity down sharply and unemployment up dramatically. Membership in the nation's labor unions
soared; by 1941 there were two and a half times as many Americans in
unions as in 1935.

From the White House on the heels of the Wagner Act came a thun-
derous barrage of insults against business. Businessmen, Roosevelt
fumed, were obstacles on the road to recovery. New strictures on the
stock market were imposed. A tax on corporate retained earnings, called
the "undistributed profits tax," was levied. "These soak-the-rich efforts,"
writes economist Robert Higgs, "left little doubt that the president and
his administration intended to push through Congress everything they
could to extract wealth from the high-income earners responsible for
making the bulk of the nation's decisions about private investment."

Higgs draws a close connection between the level of private investment and the course of the American economy in the 1930s. The relentless assaults of the Roosevelt administration—in both word and
deed—against business, property, and free enterprise guaranteed that
the capital needed to jumpstart the economy was either taxed away or
forced into hiding. When Roosevelt took America to war in 1941, he
eased up on his antibusiness agenda, but a great deal of the nation's
capital was diverted into the war effort instead of into plant expansion
or consumer goods. Not until both Roosevelt and the war were gone did
investors feel confident enough to "set in motion the postwar investment
boom that powered the economy's return to sustained prosperity."

On the eve of America's entry into World War II and twelve years after the stock market crash of Black Thursday, ten million Americans were jobless. Roosevelt had pledged in 1932 to end the crisis, but it persisted two presidential terms and countless interventions later. When federal spending collapsed and price controls were abandoned after the war, and tax rates on business were dramatically reduced in 1945, the economy began a genuine recovery.

The genesis of the Great Depression lay in the inflationary monetary policies of the U.S. government in the 1920s. It was prolonged and exacerbated by a litany of political missteps: trade-crushing tariffs, incentive-sapping taxes, mind-numbing controls on production and competition, senseless destruction of crops and cattle, and coercive labor laws, to recount just a few. It was not the free market that produced twelve years of agony; rather, it was political bungling on a scale as grand as there ever was.

(Editor's Note: This essay is condensed from the author's "Great Myths of the Great Depression," available at FEE.org).

SUMMARY

- The Great Depression did not follow a period of "unfettered capitalism." In fact, it was made inevitable by erratic monetary policy from the federal government, namely, the Federal Reserve
- After years of cheap money and low interest rates, the Fed set the stage for a correction with a policy of steep increases in interest rates and a deflation of the money supply
- The Hoover administration took a recession and made it a depression by dramatically choking off world trade through higher tariffs and doubling the income tax
- Franklin Roosevelt promised to undo Hoover's spending and tax increases but after he was elected, he did just the opposite

34

"GOVERNMENT MUST SUBSIDIZE THE ARTS"

By Lawrence W. Reed

PEOPLE WHO OPPOSE SOVIET-STYLE COLLECTIVE FARMS, GOVERNMENT SUBSIDIES to agriculture, or public ownership of grocery stores because they want the provision of food to be a private matter in the marketplace are generally not dismissed as uncivilized or uncaring. Hardly anyone would claim that one who holds such views is opposed to breakfast, lunch, and dinner. But people who oppose government funding of the arts are frequently accused of being heartless or uncultured. What follows is an adaptation of a letter I once wrote to a noted arts administrator who accused me of those very things. It articulates the case that art, like food, should rely on private, voluntary provision:

"Thanks for sending me your thoughts lamenting cuts in arts funding by state and federal governments. In my mind, however, the fact that the arts are wildly buffeted by political winds is actually a powerful case against government funding. I've always believed that art is too important to depend on politics, too critical to be undermined by politicization.

Furthermore, expecting government to pay the bill for it is a cop-out, a serious erosion of personal responsibility and respect for private property.

"Those studies that purport to show X return on Y amount of government investment in the arts are generally a laughingstock among economists. The numbers are often cooked and are almost never put alongside competing uses of public money for comparison. Moreover, a purely dollars-and-cents return—even if accurate—is a small part of the total picture.

"The fact is, virtually every interest group with a claim on the treasury argues that spending for its projects produces some magical 'multiplier' effect. Routing other people's money through the government alchemy machine is supposed to somehow magnify national wealth and income, while leaving it in the pockets of those who earned it is somehow a drag. Assuming for a moment that such preposterous claims are correct, wouldn't it make sense from a purely material perspective to calculate the average multiplier and then route all income through the government? Don't they do something like that in Cuba and North Korea? What happened to the multiplier in those places? It looks to me that somewhere along the way it became a divisor.

"What if, for instance, 'public investment' simply displaces a certain amount of private investment? (Arts subsidy advocates never raise this issue, but I know that I personally am far less likely to make a charitable contribution to something I know is on the dole than to something I know rests on the good hearts of willing givers.)

"What if 'public investment' brings with it some baggage like political manipulation that over time erodes the integrity of the recipient institutions? How does that fit into the equation?

"What if I, as a taxpayer who earned the dollars in the first place, could keep what the government would otherwise spend on the arts and invest it in my child's education and end up getting twice the return on my money that the government would ever get on the arts? The fact that you take so much from me now, by the way, means that I can purchase less of the things that I value, including such things as tickets to the theatre or a concert.

"If simply getting a good return qualifies an activity for public investment and government involvement, then I can think of hundreds of companies and industries that government 'should' have spent tax money on—from silicon chips to Berkshire Hathaway. The Constitution's framers could have dispensed with all that rigmarole about rights of citizens and duties of government and stopped with a preamble that said only, 'We the People, in order to get a high return on our tax money, establish this government to do whatever anybody can show will fetch a hefty payback.'

"Sometimes those of us who put faith in such things as the individual, private property, and the marketplace are accused of focusing solely on dollars and cents. But actually, it's those on the other side who are most guilty of this. The arts funding issue is a case in point. Advocates of government funding focus on dollars—more of them, *always* more of them—and no matter how much government funding of the arts we have, it's never enough.

"Those of us who wish to nurture the arts privately stress other, far more important values. I believe, for example, that money which comes voluntarily from the heart is much more meaningful than money that comes at gunpoint (which is ultimately what taxes are all about). You've won so much more when you convince people to do the right thing, or support the right causes, because they *want* to instead of because they *have* to. For that reason I don't believe in shotgun marriages either.

"I can think of an endless list of desirable, enriching things, very few of which carry a tag that says, 'Must be provided by taxes and politicians.' A rich culture consists, as you know, of so many good things that have nothing to do with government, and thank God they don't. We should seek to nurture those things privately and voluntarily because 'private' and 'voluntary' are key indicators that people believe in them.

"The surest way I know to sap the vitality of almost any worthwhile endeavor is to send a message that says, 'You can slack off; the government will now do it.' That sort of flight from responsibility, frankly, is at the source of many societal ills today: Many people don't take care of their parents in their old age because a federal program will do it. Most parents these days shirk their duties to educate their kids because government schools are supposed to do that (even though many of them do a miserable and expensive job of it).

"I know that art is just about everything to some people, especially those whose living derives from it. But as adults we have to resist the temptation to think that what we are individually doing is somehow the greatest thing since sliced bread and that therefore it must receive more than what people willingly give it.

"I think what my church does is important, but I don't want government giving it money. I think what we do at FEE is important, but we'd go out of business before we'd take a nickel of somebody's money against his will. I might even like certain nongovernment-funded art forms more than the ones that are politically well connected enough to get a grant, but I don't want to corrupt them with a government check. As children we want what we want and we want it now, and we don't care where it comes from or even if somebody has to be robbed for us to get it. But as discerning adults who put a higher premium on mutual respect and building a culture that rests on creativity and persuasion over coercion, we should have different standards.

"If we do not rob Peter the worker to pay Paul the artist, perhaps Paul may have to become a better artist or a better marketer of his art, or perhaps take on another profession entirely. Would that mean that we've deprived Paul of his freedom? Hardly. In a free society, Paul is always free to pursue art as either a hobby or a profession. But the same could be said of Peter, who has every right to pursue his interests too, without having his freedom diminished through taxes so that Paul's interests can be made more lucrative.

"Moreover, haven't we learned from endless, painful experiences that when you inject government money into something, you introduce politics and conflict, demagoguery and vote-buying, waste and inefficiency? Why politicize something as spontaneous and beautiful as good art? Why subsidize bad art?

"Lots of things are important in life. That doesn't mean they all need to be coercively financed. Art in its endless forms enjoys the support of nearly every human, in varying degrees (I've been in hundreds of homes and none with bare walls and no music-playing device). Claiming that the arts require the force of government is, if not self-serving, a flimsy and foolhardy assertion."

SUMMARY

- Government funding of the arts is not just music to the ears. It carries with it all the downsides of dependence on politics
- Claims that arts spending is magically "multiplied" are specious and usually self-serving, and never look at alternative uses of the same money
- Culture arises naturally and spontaneously among people who chose to interact with each other. Art is part of that, but it also competes with all sorts of other things people choose to do with their time and money
- If art is truly important, then the last thing we should want to do is politicize it or divert it toward those things that people with power think we should see or hear

35

"GOVERNMENT IS AN INFLATION FIGHTER"

By Lawrence W. Reed

"GOVERNMENT," OBSERVED THE RENOWNED AUSTRIAN ECONOMIST LUDWIG VON Mises, "is the only institution that can take a valuable commodity like paper, and make it worthless by applying ink."

Mises was describing the curse of inflation, the process whereby government expands a nation's money supply and thereby erodes the value of each monetary unit—dollar, peso, pound, euro, or whatever. It shows up in the form of rising prices, which most people confuse with the inflation itself. The distinction is important because, as economist Percy Greaves once explained so eloquently, "Changing the definition changes the responsibility."

Define inflation as rising prices and, like Jimmy Carter, you'll think that oil sheiks, credit cards, and private businesses are the culprits, and price controls are the answer. Define inflation in the classic fashion as an increase in the supply of money, with rising prices as a consequence, and you then have to ask the revealing question, "Who increases the money supply?" Only one entity can do that legally; all others are called "counterfeiters" and go to jail.

It's certainly true that many things, some beyond the control of any human being, can cause some prices to rise. A freeze in Florida, by reducing the supply of oranges at least temporarily, will prompt a spurt in orange juice prices. Bombing factories in wartime will boost the prices of whatever those factories were making. After people pay higher prices for reduced supplies, they may have less money in their pockets for buying other things, causing downward pressure on those other prices. But a prolonged, broad-based rise in most or all prices is the result of one thing: a decline in the value of money, and that occurs because whoever is producing the money is overdoing it.

Consider this analogy: Let's say you like Campbell's tomato soup so much you eat it every week. Then one week you notice that it's a little less red and doesn't taste quite as "tomatoey." A week later, it's downright pink instead of red and tastes more like water than tomatoes. Week after week this disagreeable trend continues. Would you blame consumers or would you point your finger at Campbell's, the producer? When your money buys less and less, year after year, what sense would it make to blame the people who use the stuff instead of the people who manufacture the stuff?

Most economists worth their salt have long argued that inflation is always and everywhere a monetary matter. As one of them put it, rising prices no more cause inflation than wet streets cause rain. The monetary authorities inflate and then prices rise, in that order, and if the people's confidence in that money dissipates, the price hikes will be astronomical. A little history lesson is in order.

Before paper money, governments inflated by diminishing the precious-metal content of their coinage. The ancient prophet Isaiah reprimanded the Israelites with these words: "Thy silver has become dross, thy wine mixed with water." Roman emperors repeatedly melted down the silver denarius and added junk metals until the denarius was less than 1 percent silver. The Saracens of Spain clipped the edges of their coins so they could mint more until the coins became too small to circulate. Prices rose as a mirror image of the currency's worth.

Rising prices are not the only consequence of monetary expansion. Inflation also erodes savings and encourages debt. It undermines confidence and deters investment. It destabilizes the economy by fostering booms and busts. If it's bad enough, it can even wipe out the very government responsible for it in the first place. It can lead to even worse afflictions. Hitler and Napoleon both rose to power in part because of the chaos of runaway inflations.

All this raises many issues economists have long debated and about which I have my own views. Who or what should determine a nation's supply of money? Why do governments so regularly mismanage it? What is the connection between fiscal and monetary policy? Suffice it to say here that governments inflate because their appetite for revenue exceeds their willingness to tax or their ability to borrow. British economist John Maynard Keynes was an influential charlatan in many ways, but he nailed it when he wrote, "By a continuing process of inflation, governments can confiscate, secretly and unobserved, an important part of the wealth of their citizens."

At varying rates, the unbacked (or "fiat") paper money issued by government central banks has been falling in value all over the world for decades. Even the U.S. dollar is worth about a nickel of its value in 1914, the first full year of operation of its monopoly issuer, the Federal Reserve. In recent years, perhaps no place was more ravaged by inflation than Zimbabwe in southern Africa. Prices there rocketed upwards at an annual rate exceeding 11 million percent in 2007. After printing trillions of Zimbabwean dollars to finance its socialist schemes, the Mugabe dictatorship ruined the currency utterly.

South America is home to many serial inflationists—corrupt, crackpot regimes that destroy one paper money after another. Prices in Argentina and Venezuela, for example, are currently climbing between 50 and 100 percent annually, and all indications are that the rates will accelerate in coming months.

In April 1985 I visited Bolivia to observe the world's then-highest rate of price hikes, an astonishing 50,000 percent. After stiffing its foreign creditors in the early 1980s, the government in La Paz could only finance its bad habits through taxing its own people and printing paper money. It did lots of both. By 1985, however, only 10 percent of its spending was covered by taxes; the rest was taken care of by the printing press. Paper money became the country's third largest import. Its own presses couldn't keep up with the government's demands, so planeloads of the stuff were flown in every week from Europe.

On the day I arrived, the Bolivian peso traded at 150,000 to the dollar. Just days later, it had sunk to 200,000. I brought nine million pesos home with me—a million pesos (in 1,000-peso notes) in each of nine wads bound together with string by a local bank. I kept one million, which I have to this day, and sold the other eight to gold bugs and currency collectors for $500 each. Not bad, considering that, at 200,000 to the buck, I paid just $5 for each million-peso wad ($45 for the whole nine million). That little bit of international arbitrage financed my trip, incidentally.

Bolivian hyperinflation ended just four months later, in August 1985, after the socialist government that engineered it was ousted. It had printed pesos until they were worth less than the ink and paper.

So, you say, inflation may be nasty business but it's just the really rotten few that do it. Not so. The late Frederick Leith-Ross, a famous authority on international finance, observed: "Inflation is like sin; every government denounces it and every government practices it." Even Americans have witnessed hyperinflations that destroyed two currencies—the ill-fated continental dollar of the Revolutionary War and the doomed Confederate money of the Civil War.

Today's slow-motion dollar depreciation, with prices rising at persistent but mere single-digit rates, is just a limited version of the same process. Government spends, runs deficits, and pays some of its bills through the inflation tax. How long it can go on is a matter of speculation, but trillions in national debt and public officials who get elected by making promises they don't want to pay for are not factors that should encourage us. Government is not an inflation fighter. In a world of deficit budgets, out-of-control public sector spending and debt, and pie-in-the-sky promises that government will give you just about everything, government is an inflation factory.

So it is that inflation is very much with us and is arguably one of the inevitable consequences of government run amok. But it's not a permanent, sustainable policy. It must end someday. A currency's value is not bottomless. Its erosion must cease either because government stops its reckless printing or prints until it wrecks the money. Surely, which way it concludes will depend in large measure on whether its victims come to understand what it is and where it comes from.

SUMMARY

- When you change the definition of "inflation," you change the responsibility for it
- Inflation is not rising prices. In fact, you have inflation first and then as one of the consequences, you get rising prices. Inflation, properly defined, involves an increase in the supply of money
- Historically, the more control government exerts over money, the more likely the money will lose its value. The more that government spends and doesn't pay for with tax revenue, the more likely it will resort to the printing press
- It's far more accurate to think of government as an inflation factory, not an inflation fighter

36

"OUTSOURCING IS BAD FOR THE ECONOMY"

By Tyler Watts

IN THE 2012 ELECTION, PRESIDENT OBAMA RELEASED ADS ACCUSING OPPONENT Mitt Romney of "shipping jobs overseas" as CEO of a private-equity firm, Bain Capital. Romney responded not by denying this aspect of Bain's operations, but rather by insisting that he was no longer actively managing the company at the time the alleged outsourcing occurred.

I can understand why a politician would downplay such charges. After all, "the economy" is almost always a top election issue. Many voters buy into the rhetoric that companies involved in outsourcing are somehow responsible for a net loss of employment opportunities in the United States.

Far from being a cause of economic trouble, outsourcing is actually part of any highly developed market economy. Outsourcing, in a fundamental sense, is the source of all wealth.

To tackle the misconceptions surrounding this controversy, let's start with a definition. Outsourcing means "hiring foreign workers to do a particular task, as opposed to hiring domestic workers." Now why would an entrepreneur do this? It should be pretty obvious that the foreign labor costs less. Outsourcing therefore generates some combination of lower prices for the company's products and higher profits for its owners—indicating that the company is creating more value with the resources it uses. So, as a corporate executive might say in defense of an outsourcing announcement, "it just makes economic sense for our customers and shareholders."

But what about the workers? The media focus on the horrid "shipping American jobs overseas" aspect of outsourcing. Even if they acknowledge the gains for consumers (lower prices) and shareholders (higher business profits), many commentators will complain these are offset by the losses to American workers.

First off, let's recognize that, in a free society, workers aren't entitled to their jobs; most employment is an arrangement subject to termination by either party at any time for any reason. Individual workers are always losing jobs for all manner of reasons and finding new ones—even in a recession. The mass layoffs associated with outsourcing are not economically different, just more noticeable, and therefore more subject to political demagoguery—especially in a recession.

We shouldn't ignore this kind of labor upheaval, whatever its cause. There is obviously going to be some pain associated with the adjustment process. It's never easy for people to find new employment opportunities, let alone a large pool of workers released onto the market at the same time. Readjustment costs are especially acute for people with strong local ties, such as family obligations. Underwater mortgages make it difficult for some people to migrate. Retraining for new industries is especially tough for older folks, and so on. Sad stories abound, which politicians artfully manipulate in order to enact laws and programs aimed at interrupting the normal market process in order to "save American jobs."

But economic change happens for a reason. In a free market, when outsourcing becomes viable, market forces are telling entrepreneurs, workers, and resource owners, essentially, "The old ways of doing things, the old places, the old patterns that you were so accustomed to—they're not working so well anymore. There are better ways, better places, and better patterns available. For the good of all mankind, to take advantage of the greatest possible global opportunities, we need some rearranging. A large group of people in place Z will now be able to do what people in place F used to do, but at lower costs. That means people in F need to find something else to do, whether that involves moving to place Q, joining industry Y, retraining, or what-have-you."

Of course the market is not a person and has no motives. What we call markets are just the systematic patterns of exchange, production, and specialization that take place between and among countless individuals across the world. Yet the core insight of economics is that while people tend to pursue only their own narrow interests, "market forces" act as if they are trying to maximize the value of what is being produced across the entire market space—in our case, the whole world. Long-distance business transactions are a natural and important part of this market process. It's only labeled "outsourcing" when it's done by a large corporation and involves a noticeable transfer of a certain production process across an arbitrary national boundary. The term invokes images of Gordon Gekko-like corporate executives in smoke-filled boardrooms, chuckling about the fat profits to be had by transferring widget production from Chicago to Shanghai.

But in reality all economic advances involve one form or another of outsourcing. We're all doing it all the time. When a shopper selects German beer or Colombian coffee, few people accuse her of outsourcing (hardcore "buy-local" activists notwithstanding). Yet the consumer is engaging in trade in which some production took place in a far-off location. Is it any less outsourcing when I go online and buy a book from Boston, or a suit from Seattle? Outsourcing is everywhere!

Consider what a world of no outsourcing would look like. Everything you use—and I mean everything!—must be acquired within a few miles of where you live. As economist Russ Roberts said, we've already tried that. It was called the Middle Ages, and life was "nasty, brutish, and short." Indeed, economic progress in recent centuries has been marked by ever-increasing outsourcing—what Adam Smith called an ever-extending "division of labor." We have outsourced most of our food production from the field behind our own huts to the huge farms of the corn and wheat belts, with their great farming machinery, genetic engineering, and chemical marvels, themselves all dependent on highly specialized production processes that are outsourced across the globe.

We outsourced our clothing needs from the backyard flock and the spinning wheel to the textile mill, which itself was progressively outsourced from northern England in the 1700s to New England in the 1800s, then to the southern United States in the early 1900s, and presently to parts of Asia. We outsourced entertainment from the occasional village troubadour to the big recording studios and now, with the Internet, to specialists all over the world.

I could go on, but you get the point: Throughout history the rise in outsourcing has paralleled a rise in productivity, a rise in human opportunities and accomplishments, and a rise in global living standards. This is not a coincidence; economics indicates that outsourcing is not a bane to our economic health, but a core component of economic progress.

Nothing said here, however, is meant to countenance the many government interventions, here and abroad, that distort the patterns of global commerce, making them different from those the free market would have generated.

Economics makes clear that outsourcing is not the problem; the problem is scarcity. Outsourcing is (part of) the solution. Presidential candidates or anyone interested in promoting economic progress should think about policy changes that would allow American entrepreneurs, workers, and resource owners to better integrate themselves into an increasingly interconnected global economy.

(Editor's Note: This article first appeared in FEE's magazine, The Freeman, *in November 2012.)*

SUMMARY

- Outsourcing occurs when people shop around for the best deals; we do it all the time as consumers. If it produces savings, those savings can be utilized for the purchase of other things
- Outsourcing boosts productivity and living standards. Stopping it means compelling "shoppers" (in this case, businesses) to settle for a more costly or less desirable option

37

"IF FDR'S NEW DEAL DIDN'T END THE DEPRESSION, THEN WORLD WAR II DID"

BY BURTON W. FOLSOM

WHAT FINALLY ENDED THE GREAT DEPRESSION? THAT QUESTION MAY BE THE MOST important in economic history. If we can answer it, we can better grasp what perpetuates economic stagnation and what cures it.

The Great Depression was the worst economic crisis in U.S. history. From 1931 to 1940 unemployment was always in double digits. In April 1939, almost ten years after the crisis began, more than one in five Americans still could not find work.

On the surface, World War II seems to mark the end of the Great Depression. During the war more than 12 million Americans were sent into the military, and a similar number toiled in defense-related jobs. Those war jobs seemingly took care of the 17 million unemployed in 1939. Most historians have therefore cited the massive spending during wartime as the event that ended the Great Depression.

Many economists have wisely challenged that conclusion. Let's be blunt. If the recipe for economic recovery is putting tens of millions of people in defense plants or military marches, then having them make or drop bombs on our enemies overseas, the value of world peace is called into question. In truth, building tanks and feeding soldiers—necessary as it was to winning the war—became a crushing financial burden. We merely traded debt for unemployment. The expense of funding World War II hiked the national debt from $49 billion in 1941 to almost $260 billion in 1945. In other words, the war had only postponed the issue of recovery.

Even President Roosevelt and his New Dealers sensed that war spending was not the ultimate solution; they feared that the Great Depression—with more unemployment than ever—would resume after Hitler and Hirohito surrendered. Yet FDR's team was blindly wedded to the federal spending that (as I argue in my 2009 book *New Deal or Raw Deal?*) had perpetuated the Great Depression during the 1930s.

FDR had halted many of his New Deal programs during the war—and he allowed Congress to kill the WPA, the CCC, the NYA, and others—because winning the war came first. In 1944, however, as it became apparent that the Allies would prevail, he and his New Dealers prepared the country for his New Deal revival by promising a second bill of rights. Included in the President's package of new entitlements was the right to "adequate medical care," a "decent home," and a "useful and remunerative job." These rights (unlike free speech and freedom of religion) imposed obligations on other Americans to pay taxes for eyeglasses, "decent" houses, and "useful" jobs, but FDR believed his second bill of rights was an advance in thinking from what the Founders had conceived.

Roosevelt's death in the last year of the war prevented him from unveiling his New Deal revival. But President Harry Truman was on board for most of the new reforms. In the months after the end of the war Truman gave major speeches showcasing a full employment bill—with jobs and spending to be triggered if people failed to find work in the private sector. He also endorsed a national health care program and a federal housing program.

But 1946 was very different from 1933. In 1933 large Democratic majorities in Congress and public support gave FDR his New Deal, but stagnation and unemployment persisted. By contrast, Truman had only a small Democratic majority—and no majority at all if you subtract the more conservative southern Democrats. Plus, the failure of FDR's New Deal left fewer Americans cheering for an encore.

In short the Republicans and southern Democrats refused to give Truman his New Deal revival. Sometimes they emasculated his bills; other times they just killed them.

Senator Robert Taft of Ohio, one of the leaders of the Republican-southern Democrat coalition, explained why he voted against much of the program: "The problem now is to get production and employment. If we can get production, prices will come down by themselves to the lowest point justified by increased costs. If we hold prices at a point where no one can make a profit, there will be no expansion of existing industry and no new industry in that field."

Robert Wason, president of the National Association of Manufacturers, simply said, "The problem of our domestic economy is the recovery of our freedom."

Alfred Sloan, the chairman of General Motors, framed the question this way: "Is American business in the future as in the past to be conducted as a competitive system? He answered: "General Motors...will not participate voluntarily in what stands out crystal clear at the end of the road—a regimented economy."

Taft, Wason and Sloan reflected the views of most congressmen, who proceeded to squelch the New Deal revival. Instead they cut tax rates to encourage entrepreneurs to create jobs for the returning veterans.

After many years of confiscatory taxes, businessmen desperately needed incentives to expand. By 1945 the top marginal income tax rate was 94 percent on all income over $200,000. We also had a high excess-profits tax that had absorbed more than one-third of all corporate profits since 1943—and another corporate tax that reached as high as 40 percent on other profits.

In 1945 and 1946 Congress repealed the excess-profits tax, cut the corporate tax to a maximum 38 percent, and cut the top income tax rate to 86 percent. In 1948 Congress sliced the top marginal rate further, to

82 percent. Those rates were still high, but they were the first cuts since the 1920s and sent the message that businesses could keep much of what they earned. The year 1946 was not without ups and downs in employment, occasional strikes, and rising prices. But the "regime certainty" of the 1920s had largely returned, and entrepreneurs believed they could invest again and be allowed to make money. As Sears, Roebuck and Company Chairman Robert E. Wood observed, after the war "we were warned by private sources that a serious recession was impending.... I have never believed that any depression was in store for us."

With freer markets, balanced budgets, and lower taxes, Wood was right. Unemployment was only 3.9 percent in 1946, and it remained at roughly that level during most of the next decade. The Great Depression was over.

(Editor's Note: This essay was first published in FEE's magazine, The Freeman, *in February 2010.)*

SUMMARY

- Wars aren't cures for depressions. They simply divert manpower and resources away from what consumers want to what government wants to win the conflict
- FDR's "New Deal" prolonged the depression and fortunately, attempts to revive it to keep the economy going after World War II were squelched
- The economy didn't collapse after WWII because reductions in federal spending and taxation encouraged entrepreneurship

38

"THE MINIMUM WAGE HELPS THE POOR"

BY LAWRENCE W. REED

THE ANCIENT SAGE SOCRATES, A GIANT IN THE FOUNDATION OF WESTERN PHILOSOPHY, was known for a teaching style by which he aggressively questioned his students. He employed his "Socratic method" as a way to stimulate logical, analytical thought in place of emotive or superficial pronouncement. Rather than lecture or pontificate, he would essentially interrogate. The result was to force his Greek pupils to see the full implications of their conclusions or to realize that what they had accepted as solid was nothing more than the intellectual equivalent of crumbled feta.

In his 2014 and 2015 State of the Union speeches, President Obama called upon the U.S. Congress to enact a hike in the hourly minimum wage from $7.25 to $10.10. (The dime may have been added because a nice round number without a decimal would sound unscientific.) Economists have long argued that raising the *cost* of labor, especially for small and start-up businesses, reduces the *demand* for labor (as with anything else). But progressives routinely call for increases in the minimum wage—with the usual, oversized measure of self-righteous breast-beating about helping workers. Maybe what is needed is not another lecture on the minimum wage from an economist, but rather an old-fashioned Socratic inquisition. If the old man himself were with us, here's how I imagine one such dialogue might go:

Socrates: So you want to raise the minimum wage. Why?

Citizen: Because as President Obama says, minimum wage workers haven't had a raise in five years.

Socrates: Can you name one single worker who was making $7.25 five years ago who is still making $7.25 today? And if you can't, then please tell me what caused their wage to rise if Congress didn't do it. Come on, can you name just one?

Citizen: I don't happen to have a name on me, but they must be out there somewhere.

Socrates: Well, we've just been through a deep recession because successive administrations from both parties, plus lawmakers and your friends at the Fed, created a massive bubble and jawboned banks to extend easy credit. The bust forced many businesses to cut back or close. Now we have the weakest recovery in decades as ever-higher taxes, regulations, and Obamacare stifle growth. No wonder people are hurting! Do you take any responsibility for that, or do you just issue decrees that salve your guilty conscience?

Citizen: That's water over the dam. I'm looking to the future.

Socrates: But how can you see even six months into a murky future when you refuse to look into the much clearer and more recent past? You guys think the world starts when a problem arises, as if you're incapable of analyzing the problem's origin. Maybe that's why you rarely solve a problem; you just set everybody up to repeat it. If you really look to the future, then why didn't you see this situation coming?

Citizen: Look, in any event, $7.25 just isn't enough for anybody to live on. Workers must have more to meet their basic needs.

Socrates: An employer doesn't have anything to pay an employee except what he first gets from paying customers. I wonder, whose "needs" do *you* consider when you decide to buy or not to buy: the workers' or your own? Have you ever offered to pay more than the asking price just to help out the guy who made the product? And if customers like you won't do that, where do you expect the employer to get the money?

Citizen: That's not a fair question. My intent here is purely to help.

Socrates: Sounds to me like the answer is "no," but let's move on. Why do you assume your intentions mean more to a worker than those of his employer? It's the employer who's taking the risk to offer him a job, not you. You're only making speeches about it. Don't you see a little hypocrisy here—you, who are personally offering no one a job, self-righteously criticizing others who are actually creating jobs and paying wages even if they're not all at a wage you like?

Citizen: Employers are interested only in profits.

Socrates: Are you saying employees are not? Are they more interested in working for companies that lose money, and if so, then why don't they all line up for government jobs?

Citizen: Well, government "loses" money almost every year in the sense that it spends more than it takes in, and there are plenty of people who are happy to work for it.

Socrates: But government has a printing press. It also has a legal monopoly on force. When it borrows in the capital markets, it shoves itself to the head of the line at everybody else's expense. Are you saying these are good things and that we'd be better off if the private sector could do these things too? Try to keep up with me here.

Citizen: I repeat, employers are interested only in profits. People before profits, I say! I even have a bumper sticker on my car that says that.

Socrates: So are you saying that employers would be better people if, instead of seeking profits, they tried to break even or run at a loss? How does that add value to the economy or encourage risk-takers to start a business in the first place?

Citizen: You're trying to belittle me but I went to a state university. All of my sociology, political science and gender studies professors told us that raising the minimum wage is good.

Socrates: Were any of those tenured, insulated, and government-funded pontificators actual job-creating, payroll tax-paying entrepreneurs themselves, ever?

Citizen: That's beside the point.

Socrates: *(Sigh.)* Figures.

Citizen: Look, $10.10 isn't much. I think you must be mean-spirited and greedy if you don't want people to be paid at least $10.10.

Socrates: Yeah, like the guys in government check their personal ambitions at the door when they take office. I'd like to know how you arrived at that number. Was it some sophisticated equation, divine revelation or toss of the dice? Why didn't you choose $20.00, which is not only a nice round number but also a lot more generous?

Citizen: Well, $20.00 would be too high, for sure. Too much of a jump at once.

Socrates: It sounds like you think the cost of labor might indeed affect the demand for it. Good! That's progress. You're not as oblivious about market forces as I thought. What I want to know is why you apparently don't think higher labor costs matter when you raise the minimum wage from $7.25 to $10.10. Do you think everyone, regardless of skill level or experience, is automatically worth what Congress decrees? Do you believe in magic, too? How about tooth fairies?

Citizen: Now hold on a minute. I'm for the worker here.

Socrates: Then why on earth would you favor a law that says if a worker can't find a job that pays at least $10.10 per hour, he's not allowed to work?

Citizen: I'm not saying he can't work! I'm saying he can't be paid less than $10.10!

Socrates: I thought we were making progress, but perhaps not. Can you tell me, if your scheme becomes law, what happens to a worker whose labor is worth only, say, $8.10 because of his low skills, lack of education, scant experience, or a low demand for the work itself? Will employers happily employ him anyway and take a $2.00 loss for every hour he's on the job?

Citizen: Businesses need workers and $2.00 isn't much, so common sense and decency would suggest that of course they would.

Socrates: So employers who employ people are too greedy to pay $10.10 unless they're ordered to, but then when Congress acts, they suddenly become generous enough to hire people at a loss. Who was your logic instructor?

Citizen: Can we hurry this up? I've got other plans for other people I have to think about.

Socrates: OK, just one last question. Which is better, a job at $8.50 per hour or no job at all at $10 per hour. Simple math here. Pick one.

Citizen: A nice job at $10 per hour.

Socrates: I give up. You progressives are incorrigible. You're the only people on whom my teaching method has no discernible impact. It seems that logic, evidence and economics count for nothing as long as you feel good about your intentions.

Citizens: You ask too many questions.

At this point, in utter frustration, Socrates drinks the hemlock—or at least he does in this imaginary episode.

As an economist, I wish that raising people's wages were as simple and easy as waving a wand or passing a law but that's just not the way the world works.

(Editor's Note: A version of this essay was previously published in FEE's magazine, The Freeman, *in February 2014.)*

SUMMARY

- Millions of people who are utterly unaffected by the minimum wage because they are already earning something higher to begin with see their wages rise almost every year— some even during recessions. It's not a decree of Congress that does this; it's factors such as productivity, capital investment and competition in the labor market
- You can't expect employers to pay workers more than their productivity is worth just because Congress demands it. At

higher prices (or wages), less is purchased. That's a law of economics more powerful than a minimum wage law from Congress

- If raising the minimum wage to $10.10 makes sense, why stop there? Why not declare that everyone must be paid $50/hour?

39

"FREE MARKETS EXPLOIT WOMEN"

By Anne Rathbone Bradley

A GROWING DEBATE IN THE UNITED STATES IS THAT WORKING WOMEN ARE exploited by a free labor market where they are paid, on average, significantly less than their male counterparts. Followed by this assertion is the conclusion that capitalism exacerbates the gender-wage gap and exploits women. As Curly, one of the Three Stooges, said in a famous skit, "I resemble that remark!"

As a female economist in a male-dominated field, I am sympathetic to these concerns and most certainly know that while no markets are perfect, freed markets have done the best to help women increase their skills, education and overall comparative advantage as well as to allow them a space to offer their skills in the service of others.

How does this happen and what's the evidence?

Let's start with the mechanics of how freed labor markets offer the best opportunities for women to prosper. The first necessary condition is equality before the law. In a world where women are not equal before the law and are not allowed to even show up for certain types or sectors of employment, the supply of labor is constrained. There are simply fewer people available to offer their labor when we eliminate half of the potential workforce. This has extremely negative and culturally-discriminatory effects and it also thwarts economic freedom. Firms aren't as productive as they could be. It took hundreds of years for this to be established in the United States. In many countries women are still not equal and often held hostage under the law. For example, in Saudi Arabia it is illegal for women to drive and all women are required to have a male guardian, thus making work and employment costly and difficult. It is no accident that without equality before the law, Saudi Arabia ranks 127th of 136 in gender-wage parity.

The second necessary condition is a fluid supply of labor. That is, people need to be free to choose their profession. Those professions cannot be mired down with excessive regulatory burdens that act as barriers to entering the labor force. For example, needless licensing, excessive taxation, and burdensome regulations stifle entrepreneurship and labor participation. Making it costly to enter the labor force constrains economic growth and personal prosperity. When the process of competition unfolds, those who offer salaries in exchange for labor are forced to compete with other firms who are bidding for the same labor. In a society where women are free under the law to pursue employment in industries without excessive barriers to entry, what we see is a great equalization of pay between men and women.

What's the evidence?

It is only when individuals can claim and keep the income we make without restriction that we can prosper. A freed labor market is precisely what allows this to happen. It has been empirically proven to be the best opportunity for women to unleash their creative talents on the world. It is why I got to choose to enter a math-heavy, male-dominated, PhD program. I was free under the law to choose my pursuit and it was then up to me to see if I could do it. I didn't have to bribe anyone or have a male guardian or jump through gender-biased regulatory hoops. I just had to show up and do the hard work—with no guarantee of success.

What is the result of a largely freed labor market? The most recent Bureau of Labor Statistics report suggests that the result is an increasing trajectory of wage equality. Most of the 17.9 percent wage gap in the United States can be explained by number of hours worked, marriage and age. Women who work full-time and who have never married make 95.2 percent of male earnings narrowing the gender-wage gap to less than five percent. Married women with children work fewer hours which accounts for a large portion of the wage gap.

The structure of the family is changing, including women having fewer children because of not having to worry about many children dying at birth or at very young ages, as was the case just a couple centuries ago. It is one thing to decide to have a big family, it's another to have to have a big family because of death and the need to produce labor to work for the food you will eat. As prosperity has increased, the United States is wealthier, which gives women more direct control over how they will pursue employment.

Institutions are changing as well. Now, more than ever, there are more options for tele-work and flexible hours which give women even more options as they make their own choices and manage the opportunity costs of family and work life. The bottom line is that the more women can voluntarily choose how much to work and when, the freer they are to pursue their chosen ends whether that choice is to stay at home with a large family or manage a full-time, corporate career. What is certain is for those women who want to work many paid hours and invest highly in education, there are more income opportunities in the highest quintiles than there ever have been.

Nonetheless, as St. Lawrence University economist Steven Horwitz argues in "Markets and the Gender Wage Gap," available on FEE.org, some good reasons exist for what some are quick to label "discrimination":

> Men who go to college are more likely to have majors that generate higher pay (such as computer science and engineering), while women tend toward psychology and education,

which do not pay as well. Women are more likely than men to interrupt their careers to care for children. Women (and men) who do so tend to fall behind their cohort in job experience and in keeping current in their profession. Their wages thereby fall behind their cohort's and are lower than they would have been had they not cared for the kids. All choices that affect human capital also affect wages, so discrimination in the marketplace is not required to explain pay differentials.

Forbes reported in 2014 that there have never been as many Fortune 500 female CEOs as there are now—24 in total, and that is up 4 in just one year, so the future for women business leaders is bright. In my own graduate program, there have never been more talented women pursuing PhDs as there are now, and they are completing their degrees and getting incredible academic placements.

The hope for women everywhere is equality before the law and a freed labor market. Does some institutional discrimination still exist? Of course, but the quest for profit among firms makes them accountable to market signals about hiring the best employee for the job at hand. Over time, this reduces discrimination by penalizing it (employers who engage in it lose valuable employees to competing businesses and opportunities). A freer world is a better world for everyone.

SUMMARY

- The freer the market, the more opportunities there are for women (and anyone else, for that matter) to progress up the economic ladder
- Most of the 17.9 percent wage gap in the United States can be explained by number of hours worked, marriage and age. Women who work full-time and who have never married make 95.2 percent of male earnings narrowing the gender-wage gap to less than 5 percent

- For those women who want to work many paid hours and invest highly in education, there are more income opportunities in the highest quintiles than there ever have been

40

"THE RICH ARE GETTING RICHER AND THE POOR ARE GETTING POORER"

BY MAX BORDERS

IMAGINE YOU COULD GO BACK IN TIME 50 YEARS. SUPPOSE THE REASON YOU ARE doing so is to put policies into place that would ensure that the rich got richer and the poor got poorer. (Why anyone would want to do this is beside the point, but stay with me.) What policies would you set?

1. You would want to price poor, unskilled people out of the labor market with an ever-increasing minimum wage.
2. You would provide special favors, artificial competitive advantages, and taxpayer subsidies to the politically well-connected (i.e., those already rich).
3. You would stifle new, small businesses with stacks of regulations and bureaucratic paperwork.
4. You would (literally) pay people to stay in poverty, to be dependent on government, so that any work ethic would be suppressed and eroded.

5. You would implement an erratic and largely inflationary monetary policy that erodes savings and creates destructive booms and busts.
6. You would want to soak "the rich" so as to reduce investment and the incentive of the non-rich to get wealthier.

All six of these in combination might do the trick. Throw up barriers to the progress of the poor, or pay people to stay poor, or rig the system so the rich and politically well-connected get artificial economic advantages and chances are, the poor will indeed get poorer and the rich will get richer.

By now you have probably noticed that every one of the policies above has been implemented to varying degrees during and since the Great Society. And yet *the poor have still not gotten poorer* in the United States.

According to professional skeptic Michael Shermer:

> The top-fifth income earners in the U.S. increased their share of the national income from 43 percent in 1979 to 48 percent in 2010, and the top 1 percent increased their share of the pie from 8 percent in 1979 to 13 percent in 2010. But note what has not happened: the rest have not gotten poorer. They've gotten richer: the income of the other quintiles increased by 49, 37, 36 and 45 percent, respectively.

Detractors will try to argue that the poorest quintiles have a smaller percentage of the overall pie. And that might be true, but the pie is much, much bigger. Would you rather have 50 percent of a million or 20 percent of a billion? Another way of putting this is: Would you rather be better off, even if that meant certain people were super well off? Or would you rather everyone were worse off, as long as everyone were relatively equal?

That the poorest among us are still, on balance, doing better today than they were 50 years ago is a remarkable testimony to what relatively free people and markets can do, even as governments put up roadblocks. So if the poor aren't getting poorer, why do people say they are?

If one starts with the assumption that an equal distribution of wealth is the ultimate goal, then he or she is not terribly concerned with how much of that wealth is created to begin with. But some people, at least, understand that wealth has to be created and that when there is more wealth created the poorest among us will tend to be better off. The choice of starting points boils down then to whether one cares about distributing wealth evenly or growing overall wealth through productive activity.

One reason this particular cliché manages to hang around is that people generally take a static view of the economy. The idea is that wealth is like a giant pie, which neither grows nor shrinks, but gets carved up and distributed certain ways. So, some people end up with the false idea that the only way the rich can be richer is if part of the wealth pie is taken from the poor. From this they conclude justice demands a different distribution of the pie. Advocates of "meritocracy" believe the static pie should be divided according to talent and hard work. Advocates of "social justice" think the pie should be divided according to some concept of equality. Both are wrong, but the fundamental error is in thinking that wealth is a static pie to start with. It is not.

Wealth can better be imagined as a growing pie, or better, a growing ecosystem. Of course, wealth doesn't always grow, but it tends to—as long as people have the incentives to be productive. Merit and hard work tend to be rewarded in this growing pie, but rewards more generally accrue to *those who create value for others*.

In other words, someone who works really hard might not be rewarded if no one finds his work valuable—say, a man who digs ditches and fills them up again. Likewise, work that might be considered meritorious in an obscure academic journal might not confer any earthly good on humanity outside of the journal's four-person review committee.

Advocates of so-called social justice want the wealth pie to be divided according to an arbitrary and subjective abstraction like "fairness" or equal outcomes. But carving up wealth according to some nebulous concept of justice ignores the actual ecosystem in which people operate.

In other words, such a concept ignores the behaviors, incentives and exchanges that encourage people to be productive—i.e. to generate wealth. By distributing from rich to poor, you end up paying poorer people to be less productive, while punishing more productive people. The distribution that would flow from people making more goods and services available to all is lost by degree, making everyone worse off. If taxation and redistribution for the sake of equal outcomes makes us all worse off than we would otherwise have been, how is this social justice?

Egalitarian concepts of social justice also ignore any moral considerations that might attach to how an unequal distribution might have come about. If growing overall wealth is about people creating different degrees of value for each other, and taking different risks, then the rewards of value creation will never flow equally. Some people will make more money than others, for example, whether it's because they were smarter investors, cleverer innovators, or better organizers. The rest of us enjoy the fruits of those efforts, so we might want successful people to keep investing, innovating and organizing — even if that means they get richer. And we might want to acknowledge that they deserve what they have.

(Editor's Note: Economist Thomas Sowell has said, "Since this is an era when many people are concerned about 'fairness' and 'social justice,' what is your 'fair share' of what someone else has worked for?" I often ask this question of a redistributionist in the presence of another person and ask the former to specifically tell me how much is his 'fair share' of what the other person in our presence has earned. I'm still waiting for a satisfactory answer.)

Those of us who are not as productive (or, politically well-connected, as the case may be) still enjoy remarkable abundance in relatively free societies. In the United States, for example, all quintiles have become wealthier overall, over the last 30 years.

It is also true that there are fewer desperately poor people around the world. In only 20 years, extreme global poverty has been cut in half. That is a remarkable achievement—one that is attributable to policies of liberalization (freer markets) around the world, which progressive activists and egalitarians decry. In other words, those who say the poor are getting poorer are simply wrong. And there are hundreds of millions of people thriving today who can talk about how much better things have gotten.

More than a century and a half ago, Karl Marx and his early followers claimed the rich were getting richer and the poor were getting poorer. They argued this would continue and worsen. No one in his right mind can look back on the intervening years and believe the poor were better off in 1850 than they are in 2015. Just think how much more capitalism could do to alleviate the poverty that still exists if only government were to get out of its way.

SUMMARY

- Progressives should be honest and admit that the anti-free market policies they've promoted and achieved in the last half-century have disadvantaged the poor and conferred favors upon the rich and politically well-connected
- Amazingly, in spite of those policies, the poor overall are still better off than they were 50 years ago. Imagine the progress that might have happened had these policies not been in place!
- Redistributing wealth is just slicing the pie differently, at the risk of shrinking the pie. It's a static view of wealth, one that's greatly inferior to a view of baking a bigger pie for everybody

41

"ROCKEFELLER'S STANDARD OIL COMPANY PROVED WE NEEDED ANTITRUST LAWS TO FIGHT MARKET MONOPOLIES"

BY LAWRENCE W. REED

AMONG THE GREAT MISCONCEPTIONS ABOUT A FREE ECONOMY IS THE WIDELY-HELD belief that "laissez-faire" embodies a natural tendency toward monopoly concentration. Under unfettered capitalism, so goes the familiar refrain, large firms would systematically devour smaller ones, corner markets, and stamp out competition until every inhabitant of the land fell victim to their power. Supposedly, John D. Rockefeller's Standard Oil Company of the late 1800s gave substance to this perspective.

In 1899, Standard refined 90 percent of America's oil—the peak of the company's dominance of the refining business. Though that market share was steadily siphoned off by competitors after 1899, the company nonetheless has been branded ever since as "an industrial octopus."

Does the story of Standard Oil really present a case *against* the free market? In my opinion, it most emphatically does not. Furthermore, setting the record straight on this issue must become an important weapon in every free market advocate's intellectual arsenal.

Theoretically, there are two kinds of monopoly: coercive and efficiency. A coercive monopoly results from, in the words of Adam Smith, "a government grant of exclusive privilege." Government, in effect, must take sides in the market in order to give birth to a coercive monopoly. It must make it difficult, costly, or impossible for anyone but the favored firm to do business.

The United States Postal Service is an example of this kind of monopoly. By law, no one can deliver first class mail except the USPS. Fines and imprisonment (coercion) await all those daring enough to compete. *(Editor's Note: In the years since this article was written, technology in the form of fax machines, overnight delivery services, the Internet and e-mail have allowed the private sector to get around the government monopoly in traditional, first-class mail delivery.)*

In some other cases, the government may not ban competition outright, but simply bestow privileges, immunities, or subsidies on one firm while imposing costly requirements on all others. Regardless of the method, a firm which enjoys a coercive monopoly is in a position to harm the consumer and get away with it.

An efficiency monopoly, on the other hand, earns a high share of a market because it does the best job. It receives no special favors from the law to account for its size. Others are free to compete and, if consumers so will it through their purchases, to grow as big as the "monopoly."

An efficiency monopoly has no legal power to compel people to deal with it or to protect itself from the consequences of its unethical practices. It can only attain bigness through its excellence in satisfying customers and by the economy of its operations. An efficiency monopoly which turns its back on the very performance which produced its success would be, in effect, posting a sign, "Competitors Wanted." The market rewards excellence and exacts a toll on mediocrity. The historical record casts the Standard Oil Company in the role of efficiency monopoly—a firm to which consumers repeatedly awarded their votes of confidence.

The oil rush began with the discovery of oil by Colonel Edwin Drake at Titusville, Pennsylvania in 1859. Northwestern Pennsylvania soon "was overrun with businessmen, speculators, misfits, horse dealers, drillers, bankers, and just plain hell-raisers. Dirt-poor farmers leased land at fantastic prices, and rigs began blackening the landscape. Existing towns jammed full overnight with 'strangers,' and new towns appeared almost as quickly."

In the midst of chaos emerged young John D. Rockefeller. An exceptionally hard-working and thrifty man, Rockefeller transformed his early interest in oil into a partnership in the refinery stage of the business in 1865.

Five years later, Rockefeller formed the Standard Oil Company with 4 per cent of the refining market. Less than thirty years later, he reached that all-time high of 90 per cent. What accounts for such stunning success?

On December 30, 1899, Rockefeller was asked that very question before a governmental investigating body called the Industrial Commission. He replied:

> I ascribe the success of the Standard to its consistent policy to make the volume of its business large through the merits and cheapness of its products. It has spared no expense in finding, securing, and utilizing the best and cheapest methods of manufacture. It has sought for the best superintendents and workmen and paid the best wages. It has not hesitated to sacrifice old machinery and old plants for new and better ones. It has placed its manufactories at the points where they could supply markets at the least expense. It has not only sought markets for its principal products, but for all possible by-products, sparing no expense in introducing them to the public. It has not hesitated to invest millions of dollars in methods of cheapening the gathering and distribution of oils by pipe lines, special cars, tank steamers, and tank wagons. It has erected tank stations at every important railroad station to cheapen the storage and delivery of its products.

Rockefeller was a managerial genius—a master organizer of men as well as of materials. He had a gift for bringing devoted, brilliant, and hard-working young men into his organization. Among his most out-standing associates were H. H. Rogers, John D. Archbold, Stephen V. Harkness, Samuel Andrews, and Henry M. Flagler. Together they emphasized efficient economic operation, research, and sound financial practices.

Socialist historian Gabriel Kolko, who argues in *The Triumph of Conservatism* that the forces of competition in the free market of the late 1800s were too potent to allow Standard to cheat the public, stresses that "Standard treated the consumer with deference. Crude and refined oil prices for consumers declined during the period Standard exercised great-est control of the industry."

Standard's service to the consumer in the form of lower prices is well-documented. Professor D. T. Armentano notes:

> Between 1870 and 1885 the price of refined kerosene dropped from 26 cents to 8 cents per gallon. In the same period, the Standard Oil Company reduced the [refining] costs per gallon from almost 3 cents in 1870 to 0.452 cents in 1885. Clearly, the firm was relatively efficient, and its efficiency was being translated to the consumer in the form of lower prices for a much improved product, and to the firm in the form of addi-tional profits.

That story continued for the remainder of the century, with the price of kerosene to the consumer falling to 5.91 cents per gallon in 1897. Armentano concludes from the record that "at the very pinnacle of Stan-dard's industry 'control,' the *costs and the prices for refined oil reached their lowest levels in the history of the petroleum industry*."

John D. Rockefeller's success, then, was a consequence of his superior performance. He derived his impressive market share not from govern-ment favors but rather from aggressive courting of the consumer. Stan-dard Oil is one of history's classic efficiency monopolies.

But what about the many serious charges leveled against Standard? Predatory price cutting? Buying out competitors? Conspiracy? Railroad rebates? Charging any price it wanted? Greed? Each of these can be viewed as an assault not just on Standard Oil but on businesses and the free market in general. They can and must be answered.

Predatory price cutting is "the practice of deliberately underselling rivals in certain markets to drive them out of business, and then raising prices to exploit a market devoid of competition." Let's see if it's a charge that holds water on just one of those one-liners progressives like to toss out whether the evidence is there or not.

In fact, Professor John S. McGee, writing in the *Journal of Law and Economics* for October 1958, stripped this charge of any intellectual substance. Describing it as "logically deficient," he concluded, "I can find little or no evidence to support it."

In research for his extraordinary article, McGee scrutinized the testimony of Rockefeller's competitors who claimed to have been victims of predatory price cutting. He found their claims to be shallow and misdirected. McGee pointed out that some of these very people later opened new refineries and successfully challenged Standard again.

Beyond the actual record, economic theory also argues against a winning policy of predatory price cutting in a free market for the following reasons:

1. *Price is only one aspect of competition.* Firms compete in a variety of ways: service, location, packaging, marketing, even courtesy. For price alone to draw customers away from the competition, the predator would have to cut substantially—enough to outweigh all the other competitive pressures the others can throw at him. That means suffering losses on every unit sold. If the predator has a war-chest of "monopoly profits" to draw upon in such a battle, then the predatory price cutting theorist must explain how he was able to achieve such ability in the absence of this practice in the first place!

2. *The large firm stands to lose the most.* By definition, the large firm is already selling the most units. As a predator, it

must actually step up its production if it is to have any effect on competitors. As Professor McGee observed, "To lure customers away from somebody, he (the predator) must be prepared to serve them himself. The monopolizer thus finds himself in the position of selling more—and therefore losing more—than his competitors."

3. *Consumers will increase their purchases at the "bargain prices."* This factor causes the predator to step up production even further. It also puts off the day when he can "cash in" on his hoped-for victory because consumers will be in a position to refrain from purchasing at higher prices, consuming their stockpiles instead.

4. *The length of the battle is always uncertain.* The predator does not know how long he must suffer losses before his competitors quit. It may take weeks, months, or even years. Meanwhile, consumers are "cleaning up" at his expense.

5. *Any "beaten" firms may reopen.* Competitors may scale down production or close only temporarily as they "wait out the storm." When the predator raises prices, they enter the market again. Conceivably, a "beaten" firm might be bought up by someone for a "song," and then, under fresh management and with relatively low capital costs, face the predator with an actual competitive cost advantage.

6. *High prices encourage newcomers.* Even if the predator drives everyone else from the market, raising prices will attract competition from people heretofore not even in the industry. The higher the prices go, the more powerful that attraction.

7. *The predator would lose the favor of consumers.* Predatory price cutting is simply not good public relations. Once known, it would swiftly erode the public's faith and good will. It might even evoke consumer boycotts and a backlash of sympathy for the firm's competitors.

In summary, let me quote Professor McGee once again:

> Judging from the Record, Standard Oil did not use predatory
> price discrimination to drive out competing refiners, nor did
> its pricing practice have that effect...I am convinced that
> Standard did not systematically, if ever, use local price cutting
> in retailing, or anywhere else, to reduce competition. To do
> so would have been foolish; and, whatever else has been said
> about them, the old Standard organization was seldom criti-
> cized for making less money when it could readily have made
> more.

A second charge is that Standard bought out its competitors. The
intent of this practice, the critics say, was to stifle competitors by absorbing them.

First, it must be said that Standard had no legal power to coerce a
competitor into selling. For a purchase to occur, Rockefeller had to pay
the *market* price for an oil refinery. And evidence abounds that he often
hired the very people whose operations he purchased. "Victimized ex-
rivals," wrote McGee, "might be expected to make poor employees and
dissident or unwilling shareholders."

Kolko writes that "Standard attained its control of the refinery business primarily by mergers, not price wars, and most refinery owners were
anxious to sell out to it. Some of these refinery owners later reopened
new plants after selling to Standard."

Buying out competitors can be a wise move if achieving economy of
scale is the intent. Buying out competitors merely to eliminate them from
the market can be a futile, expensive, and never-ending policy. It appears
that Rockefeller's mergers were designed with the first motive in mind.

Even so, other people found it profitable to go into the business of
building refineries and selling to Standard. David P. Reighard managed
to build and sell three successive refineries to Rockefeller, all on excellent
terms.

A firm which adopts a policy of absorbing others solely to stifle competition embarks upon the impossible adventure of putting out the recurring and unpredictable prairie fires of competition.

A third accusation holds that Standard secured secret agreements with competitors to carve up markets and fix prices at higher-than-market levels. I will not contend here that Rockefeller never attempted this policy. His experiment with the South Improvement Company in 1872 provides at least some evidence that he did. I do argue, however, that all such attempts were failures from the start and no harm to the consumer occurred.

Standard's price performance, cited extensively above, supports my argument. Prices fell steadily on an improving product. Some conspiracy! From the perspective of economic theory, collusion to raise and/or fix prices is a practice doomed to failure in a free market for these reasons:

1. *Internal pressures.* Conspiring firms must resolve the dilemma of production. To exact a higher price than the market currently permits, production must be curtailed. Otherwise, in the face of a fall in demand, the firms will be stuck with a quantity of unsold goods. Who will cut their production and by how much? Will the conspirators accept an equal reduction for all when it is likely that each faces a unique constellation of cost and distribution advantages and disadvantages?

   Assuming a formula for restricting production is agreed upon, it then becomes highly profitable for any member of the cartel to quietly cheat on the agreement. By offering secret rebates or discounts or other "deals" to his competitors' customers, any conspirator can undercut the cartel price, earn an increasing share of the market and make a lot of money. When the others get wind of this, they must quickly break the agreement or lose their market shares to the "cheater." The very reason for the conspiracy in the first place—higher profits—proves to be its undoing!

2. *External pressures.* This comes from competitors who are
not parties to the secret agreement. They feel under no obligation to abide by the cartel price and actually use their
somewhat lower price as a selling point to customers. The
higher the cartel price, the more this external competition
pays. The conspiracy must either convince all outsiders to
join the cartel (making it increasingly likely that somebody
will cheat) or else dissolve the cartel to meet the competition.

A fourth charge involves the matter of railroad rebates. John D.
Rockefeller received substantial rebates from railroads who hauled his
oil, a factor which critics claim gave him an unfair advantage over other
refiners.

The fact is that most all refiners received rebates from railroads. This
practice was simply evidence of stiff competition among the roads for
the business of hauling refined oil products. Standard got the biggest
rebates because Rockefeller was a shrewd bargainer and because he
offered the railroads large volume on a regular basis.

This charge is even less credible when one considers that Rockefeller
increasingly relied on his own pipelines, not railroads, to transport his
oil.

Did Standard Oil have the power to charge any price it wanted? A
fifth accusation says yes. According to the notion that Standard's size
gave it the power to charge any price, bigness per se immunizes the firm
from competition and consumer sovereignty.

As an "efficiency monopoly," Standard could not coercively prevent
others from competing with it. And others did, so much so that the
company's share of the market declined dramatically after 1899. As the
economy shifted from kerosene to electricity, from the horse to the auto-
mobile, and from oil production in the East to production in the Gulf
States, Rockefeller found himself losing ground to younger, more aggressive competitors.

Neither did Standard have the power to compel people to buy its
products. It had to rely on its own excellence to attract and keep customers.

(See chapter 13, "Cooperation, Not Competition" for a brief discussion of the factors which insure that no firm, regardless of size, can charge and get any price it wants).

It makes sense to view competition in a free market not as a static phenomenon, but as a dynamic, never-ending, leap-frog process by which the leader today can be the follower tomorrow.

The sixth charge, that John D. Rockefeller was a "greedy" man, is the most meaningless of all the attacks on him but nonetheless echoes constantly in the history books.

If Rockefeller wanted to make a lot of money (and there is no doubting he did), he certainly discovered the free market solution to his problem: produce and sell something that consumers will buy and buy again. One of the great attributes of the free market is that it channels greed into constructive directions. One cannot accumulate wealth without offering something in exchange!

At this point the reader might rightly wonder about the dissolution of the Standard Oil Trust in 1911. Didn't the Supreme Court find Standard guilty of successfully employing anti-competitive practices?

Interestingly, a careful reading of the decision reveals that no attempt was made by the Court to examine Standard's conduct or performance. The justices did not sift through the conflicting evidence concerning any of the government's allegations against the company. No specific finding of guilt was made with regard to those charges. Although the record clearly indicates that "prices fell, costs fell, outputs expanded, product quality improved, and hundreds of firms at one time or another produced and sold refined petroleum products in competition with Standard Oil," the Supreme Court ruled against the company. The justices argued simply that the competition between some of the divisions of Standard Oil was less than the competition that existed between them when they were separate companies before merging with Standard.

In 1915, Charles W. Eliot, president of Harvard, observed: "The organization of the great business of taking petroleum out of the earth, piping the oil over great distances, distilling and refining it, and distributing it in tank steamers, tank wagons, and cans all over the earth, was an American invention." Let the facts record that the great Standard Oil Company, more than any other firm, and John D. Rockefeller, more than any other man, were responsible for this amazing development.

(Editor's Note: This article first appeared in FEE's magazine, The Freeman, *in March 1980. Footnotes can be found in that version on FEE.org.)*

SUMMARY

- If the Standard Oil Company was any kind of "monopoly," it was not a "coercive" one because it did not derive its high (and temporary) market share from special government favors. There were lots of competitors to it, here and abroad. If it was a monopoly, then it was of the "efficiency" variety, meaning that it earned a high market share because consumers liked what it offered at attractive prices

- The prices of Standard products (chiefly kerosene in the company's early history) steadily fell. The quality steadily improved. Total production grew from year to year. This is not supposed to be the behavior of an evil monopolist, who supposedly restricts output and raises prices

- Accusations against Standard—predatory price cutting, buying up competitors, conspiracy to restrict output and raise prices, securing railroad rebates, etc.—sound plausible on the surface but fall apart upon close inspection

42

"JESUS CHRIST WAS A PROGRESSIVE BECAUSE HE ADVOCATED INCOME REDISTRIBUTION TO HELP THE POOR"

By Lawrence W. Reed

YOU DON'T HAVE TO BE A CHRISTIAN TO APPRECIATE THE DECEIT IN THIS CANARD.
You can be a person of any faith or no faith at all. You just have to appreciate facts.

I first heard something similar to this cliché some 40 years ago. As a Christian, I was puzzled. *I had always understood Christ's message to be that the most important decision a person would make in his earthly lifetime was to accept or reject Him as savior.* That decision was clearly to be a very personal one—an individual and voluntary choice. He constantly stressed inner, spiritual renewal as far more critical to well-being than material things. I wondered, "How could the same Christ advocate the use of force to take stuff from some and give it to others?" I just couldn't imagine Him supporting a fine or a jail sentence for people who don't want to fork over their money for food stamp programs.

"Wait a minute," you say. "Didn't He answer, 'Render unto Caesar the things that are Caesar's, and unto God the things that are God's' when the Pharisees tried to trick Him into denouncing a Roman-imposed tax?" Yes indeed, He did say that. It's found first in the Gospel of Matthew, chapter 22, verses 15-22 and later in the Gospel of Mark, chapter 12, verses 13-17. But notice that everything depends on just what did truly belong to Caesar and what didn't, which is actually a rather powerful endorsement of property rights. Christ said nothing like "It belongs to Caesar if Caesar simply says it does, no matter how much he wants, how he gets it, or how he chooses to spend it."

The fact is, one can scour the Scriptures with a fine-tooth comb and find nary a word from Christ that endorses the forcible redistribution of wealth by political authorities. None, period.

"But didn't Christ say he came to uphold the law?" you ask. Yes, in Matthew 5:17-20, he declares, "Do not think that I have come to abolish the Law or the Prophets; I have not come to abolish them but to fulfill them." In Luke 24: 44, He clarifies this when he says "...[A]ll things must be fulfilled which were written in the law of Moses, and in the prophets, and in the psalms, concerning me." He was not saying, "Whatever laws the government passes, I'm all for." He was speaking specifically of the Mosaic Law (primarily the Ten Commandments) and the prophecies of His own coming.

Consider the 8th of the Ten Commandments: "You shall not steal." Note the period after the word "steal." This admonition does not read, "You shall not steal unless the other guy has more than you do" or "You shall not steal unless you're absolutely positive you can spend it better than the guy who earned it." Nor does it say, "You shall not steal but it's OK to hire someone *else*, like a politician, to do it for you."

In case people were still tempted to steal, the 10th Commandment is aimed at nipping in the bud one of the principal motives for stealing (and for redistribution): "You shall not covet." In other words, if it's not yours, keep your fingers off of it.

In Luke 12:13-15, Christ is confronted with a redistribution request. A man with a grievance approaches him and demands, "Master, speak to my brother and make him divide the inheritance with me." The Son of God, the same man who wrought miraculous healings and calmed the waves, replies thusly: "*Man, who made me a judge or divider over you?* Take heed and beware of covetousness, for a man's wealth does not consist of the material abundance he possesses." Wow! He could have equalized the wealth between two men with a wave of His hand but he chose to denounce envy instead.

"What about the story of the Good Samaritan? Doesn't that make a case for government welfare programs, if not outright redistribution?" you inquire. The answer is an emphatic NO!" Consider the details of the story, as recorded in Luke 10:29-37: A traveler comes upon a man at the side of a road. The man had been beaten and robbed and left half-dead. What did the traveler do? He helped the man himself, on the spot, with his own resources. He did not say, "Write a letter to the emperor" or "Go see your social worker" and walk on. If he had done that, he would more likely be known today as the "Good-*for-nothing* Samaritan," if he was remembered at all.

What about the reference, in the Book of Acts, to the early Christians selling their worldly goods and sharing communally in the proceeds? That sounds like a progressive utopia. On closer inspection, however, it turns out that those early Christians did not sell everything they had and were not commanded or expected to do so. They continued to meet in their own private homes, for example. In his contributing chapter to the 2014 book, *For the Least of These: A Biblical Answer to Poverty*, Art Lindsley of the Institute for Faith, Work and Economics writes,

> Again, in this passage from Acts, there is no mention of the state at all. These early believers contributed their goods freely, without coercion, voluntarily. Elsewhere in Scripture we see that Christians are even instructed to give in just this manner, freely, for "God loves a cheerful giver" (2 Corinthians 9:7). There is plenty of indication that private property rights were still in effect....

It may disappoint progressives to learn that Christ's words and deeds repeatedly upheld such critically-important, capitalist virtues as contract, profit and private property. For example, consider His "Parable of the Talents." Of several men in the story, the one who takes his money and buries it is reprimanded while the one who invests and generates the largest return is applauded and rewarded.

Though not central to the story, good lessons in supply-and-demand as well as the sanctity of contract are apparent in Christ's "Parable of the Workers in the Vineyard." A landowner offers a wage to attract workers for a day of urgent work picking grapes. Near the end of the day, he realizes he has to quickly hire more and to get them, he offers for an hour of work what he previously had offered to pay the first workers for the whole day. When one of those who worked all day complained, the landowner answered, "I am not being unfair to you, friend. Didn't you agree to work for a denarius? Take your pay and go. I want to give the one who was hired last the same as I gave you. Don't I have the right to do what I want with my own money? Or are you envious because I am generous?"

The well-known "Golden Rule" comes from the lips of Christ Himself, in Matthew 7:12. "So in everything, do unto others what you would have them do unto you, for this sums up the Law and the Prophets." In Matthew 19:18, Christ says, "...love your neighbor as yourself." Nowhere does He even remotely suggest that we should dislike a neighbor because of his wealth or seek to take that wealth from him. If you don't want your property confiscated (and most people don't, and wouldn't need a thief in order to part with it anyway), then clearly you're not supposed to confiscate somebody else's.

Christian doctrine cautions against greed. So does present-day economist Thomas Sowell: "I have never understood why it is 'greed' to want to keep the money you have earned but *not* greed to want to take somebody else's money." Using the power of government to grab another person's property isn't exactly altruistic. Christ never even implied that accumulating wealth through peaceful commerce was in any way wrong; He simply implored people to not allow wealth to rule them or corrupt their character. That's why His greatest apostle, Paul, didn't say money was evil in the famous reference in 1 Timothy 6:10. Here's what Paul actually said: "For *the love* of money is a root of all kinds of evil. Some people, eager for money, have wandered from the faith and pierced themselves with many griefs." Indeed, progressives themselves have not selflessly abandoned money, for its *other people's money*, especially that of "the rich," that they're always clamoring for.

In Matthew 19:23, Christ says, "Truly I tell you, it will be hard for a rich person to get into the kingdom of heaven." A progressive might say, "Eureka! There it is! He doesn't like rich people" and then stretch the remark beyond recognition to justify almost any rob-Peter-to-pay-Paul scheme that comes down the pike. But this admonition is entirely consistent with everything else Christ says. It's not a call to envy the rich, to take from the rich or to give "free" cell phones to the poor. It's a call to character. It's an observation that some people let their wealth rule them, rather than the other way around. It's a warning about temptations (which come in many forms, not just material wealth). Haven't we all noticed that among the rich, as is equally true among the poor, you have both good and bad people? Haven't we all seen some rich celebrities corrupted by their fame and fortune, while others among the rich live perfectly upstanding lives? Haven't we all seen some poor people who allow their poverty to demoralize and enervate them, while others among the poor view it as an incentive to improve?

In Christ's teachings and in many other parts of the New Testament, Christians—indeed, all people—are advised to be of "generous spirit," to care for one's family, to help the poor, to assist widows and orphans, to exhibit kindness and to maintain the highest character. How all that gets translated into the dirty business of coercive, vote-buying, politically-driven redistribution schemes is a problem for prevaricators with agendas. It's not a problem for scholars of what the Bible actually says and doesn't say.

Search your conscience. Consider the evidence. Be mindful of facts. And ask yourself: "When it comes to helping the poor, would Christ prefer that you give your money freely to the Salvation Army or at gunpoint to the welfare department?

Christ was no dummy. He was not interested in the public professions of charitableness in which the legalistic and hypocritical Pharisees were fond of engaging. He dismissed their self-serving, cheap talk. He knew it was often insincere, rarely indicative of how they conducted their personal affairs, and always a dead-end with plenty of snares and delusions along the way. It would hardly make sense for him to champion the poor by supporting policies that undermine the process of wealth creation necessary to help them. In the final analysis, He would never endorse a scheme that doesn't work and is rooted in envy or theft. In spite of the attempts of many modern-day progressives to make Him into Robin Hood, He was nothing of the sort.

(Editor's Note: A substantially longer version of this essay is available at no charge as an e-book and in audio format under the title, Rendering Unto Caesar: Was Jesus a Socialist? *at FEE.org.)*

SUMMARY

- Free will, not coercion, is a central and consistent element in the teachings of Christ
- It is not recorded anywhere that Christ called for the state to use its power to redistribute wealth
- Christ endorsed things like choice, charity, generosity, kindness, personal responsibility, and voluntary association—things that are irreconcilable with coercively-financed redistribution schemes

43

"THE FREE MARKET CANNOT PROVIDE PUBLIC EDUCATION"

By Sheldon Richman

CAN THE FREE MARKET PROVIDE PUBLIC EDUCATION? THE SHORT ANSWER, OF course, is: yes, look around. Right now, private enterprise and nonprofit organizations provide all manner of education—from comprehensive schools with classes in the traditional academic subjects, to specialized schools that teach everything from the fine arts to the martial arts, from dancing to dieting, from scuba diving to scrutinizing one's inner self.

If we define "public education" as "what the government does now," then it's a trick question. Every school serves members of the public. For the sake of this discussion, we can ignore that the word "public" has been corrupted to mean "coercively financed through the tax system."

The free market—and I include here both for-profit and nonprofit organizations—would provide even more education than it does now but for the "unfair competition" from government. Since government has a resource that private organizations lack—the taxpayers—it's able to offer its services for "free." They're not really free, of course; in the government context, "free" means that everyone pays whether he wants the service or not. Clearly, as long as government can tax its citizens and then provide educational services to them at a marginal price of zero, much private education will never come into being. How ironic that government vigilantly looks for predatory pricing in the private sector when *it* is the major offender.

There is certainly nothing about education that should lead anyone to doubt that the market could provide it. Like any other product or service, education is a combination of land, labor, and capital goods directed at a particular objective—instruction in academic subjects and related matters demanded by a class of consumers, primarily parents.

Here's where things may get contentious. Critics of market-provided education are uncomfortable with education's being treated like a commodity, subject to supply and demand. In the marketplace, consumers ultimately determine what is produced. Entrepreneurs take risks to serve *them*. And fickle consumers show no mercy when something new and attractive comes along. Ask the shareholders of Boston Chicken or Kodak, among others.

Why should parents alone determine what is and what is not acceptable education? But why *not* parents? To whose hearts are the interests of children closer? Besides, most parents would no more make educational decisions without consulting knowledgeable authorities than they would make medical decisions without consulting doctors. The uninformed-consumer argument against free-market education is a red herring.

Parents, and the private sector, should be free to determine what is and what is not acceptable academic education for the same reasons they are free to determine what is proper religious education. We don't use the small number of neglectful parents as a pretext for government control or finance of religion. Nor should we use it as a pretext for government control or finance of schooling.

Defenders of government schooling have enlisted various economic arguments related to "market failure" to dispute the idea that parents in a free market should ultimately determine what educational services are offered. These arguments fail. Education does not have the characteristics of a "public good." One person's consumption of a given service can detract from another person's consumption, and nonpayers can be excluded.

Nor does the positive-externality case succeed. Education obviously does have spillover benefits, but that is not enough in economic theory to justify government action. You would have to believe that the external benefits would cause education to be under-consumed unless the government subsidized it. No one has ever shown that. Nor could anyone. To believe that, you'd have to believe that parents engage in the following reasoning: I'd like to buy X amount of education for my child, but since society will benefit by my child's erudition without paying anything for it, I'll buy less than X amount of education. Ridiculous, isn't it?

The argument that high-quality education is intrinsically too expensive for a significant portion of the population to afford also fails. A free market that can saturate society with refrigerators, microwave ovens, washing machines, and telephones—cellular and otherwise—can surely produce good education for a mass society. The key is entrepreneurship.

We think we know what education is and what methods work. And we do know some things. This sense of certainty might encourage us to think that education is best left to government. But we shouldn't be so presumptuous, or we could wind up like the nineteenth-century Patent Office official who said the office should be closed because everything useful had been invented.

The world is open-ended. We don't know exactly what we will learn tomorrow. As fallible beings, we can be sure that at any time, valuable information and opportunities are being overlooked. Scarce resources are being misdirected because our knowledge is incomplete. This is as true for education as for anything else.

What can we do to hasten the discovery and correction of error? We already have a method: entrepreneurship. What entrepreneurs do is search the landscape for instances where resources are being under-used, that is, devoted to the production of goods and services that consumers value less highly than other things those resources might be devoted to. What lures entrepreneurs to discover those instances is profit. Nothing approaches its power to stimulate discovery. Profit accrues when an alert entrepreneur, noticing what others have overlooked, switches resources from producing things consumers value less highly to producing things consumers value more highly.

The application of this principle to education should be obvious. Since we don't know today all that we may learn about educational methods and objectives tomorrow, we need entrepreneurship in education. Government isn't up to the task. Bureaucracy is the opposite of enterprise. It stifles enterprise. Government domination of education assures that the entrepreneurial innovation and creativity we are accustomed to in, say, the computer industry will be missing from education.

There is no good substitute for the decentralized, spontaneous entrepreneurial process that full privatization of education would stimulate.

Thus it is not only the case that the free market *can* provide education. We may conclude further that only the free market *should* provide education.

(Editor's Note: A version of this essay was originally published in The Freeman *magazine in June 2000.)*

SUMMARY

- As long as government can tax its citizens and then provide educational services to them at a marginal price of zero, much private education will never come into being
- Most parents would no more make educational decisions without consulting knowledgeable authorities than they would make medical decisions without consulting doctors
- We don't use the small number of neglectful parents as a pretext for government control or finance of religion. Nor should we use it as a pretext for government control or finance of schooling

- Government domination of education assures that the entrepreneurial innovation and creativity we are accustomed to in, say, the computer industry will be missing from education

44

"WARREN BUFFETT'S FEDERAL TAX RATE IS LESS THAN HIS SECRETARY'S"

By George Harbison

IN AUGUST 2011, WARREN BUFFETT WROTE AN OPINION PIECE IN THE *NEW YORK* *Times* in which he made the assertion that his 2010 "federal tax rate" of 17.4 percent was 18.6 percentage points less than the 36.0 percent average rate paid by the twenty other workers in his office.

Buffett's piece garnered substantial media attention and, in the months since its publication, his "federal tax rate" assertion has been woven into the fabric of American politics. His analysis was the basis for the "Buffett Rule," a tax plan proposed by President Obama that would implement measures under which everyone making more than $1 million in income per year would pay a minimum effective tax rate of 30 percent.

Clearly, given Buffett's status as a legendary businessman and investor (the "Oracle of Omaha"), his tax analysis carried a great deal of credibility and, as such, it was never challenged. Adding to the unchallenged acceptance of Buffett's assertion was the fact that Buffett never released (a) his 2010 federal tax return, (b) the federal tax returns of his office workers, and (c), the analysis underlying has "federal tax rate" assertion.

In truth, Buffett's assertion is completely inaccurate and is based on a fundamentally flawed analysis of basic federal taxation principles. In reality, he pays a much higher relevant "federal tax rate" than any of his office workers.

First of all, payroll taxes (Social Security and Medicare) are totally irrelevant for this type of analysis. Because these taxes were not assessed on non-wage income (prior to 2013), and because Social Security taxes were only assessed on the first $106,800 of wage income in 2010, the amount Buffett paid into these programs was very close, in dollar terms, to the amounts paid into them by each of his office workers. But because Buffett had total taxable income of almost $40 million, the amount of Social Security and Medicare taxes paid by him in 2010 represented only a tiny fraction of his total taxable income. For most of his office workers, these taxes represented 7.65 percent of their taxable income (even though they paid roughly the same amount as Buffett did in dollar terms). This 7.65 percent payroll tax differential is part of the 18.6 percent differential cited by Buffett in his op-ed.

But what Buffett failed to mention is the fact that Social Security and Medicare benefits are capped as well. Upon retirement, Buffett will receive almost exactly the same Social Security and Medicare benefits (in dollar terms) that his office workers will receive. There is very little differential between Buffett and his office workers in terms of what they pay into the Social Security and Medicare programs, and what they will receive in benefits. As such, the 7.65 percentage point "federal tax rate" differential between Buffett and his co-workers arising from the existing Social Security and Medicare taxing mechanism is simply not relevant, and is a mirage.

A second flaw in Buffett's analysis has to do with the fact that he included employer-paid payroll taxes in coming up with his and his office workers' "federal tax rates." The obvious problem here is that Buffett's co-workers do not pay these taxes. Rather, as a partial owner of Berkshire Hathaway, Buffett himself pays them. Buffett's inclusion of these taxes, paid by Berkshire Hathaway, into his analysis was clearly incorrect and it distorts the rates he cited. Of course, he included employer-paid payroll taxes to double the 7.65 percent "federal tax rate" differential mirage identified in the previous paragraph.

Buffett himself owns 33.9 percent of Berkshire Hathaway, a publicly traded corporation with taxable income of $19.1 billion in 2010. Assuming a very conservative corporate federal tax rate of 25 percent, Berkshire will ultimately pay $4.76 billion in federal corporate income taxes on this taxable income. Corporate taxes are borne by shareholders of the corporation, in that these taxes reduce the amount of cash available for (a) dividend payments (Berkshire has not historically paid dividends to its shareholders), or (b) reinvestment into the corporation in order to increase shareholder value.

Given his ownership stake in Berkshire, 33.9 percent of the $4.77 billion in federal corporate taxes, or $1.61 billion, were borne by Buffett. Buffett ignored this tax amount in compiling his "federal tax rate" analysis. If Buffett's share of corporate taxable income and corporate taxes paid are factored into his analysis, his overall 2010 "federal tax rate" increases by 7.56 percentage points, from 17.4 percent to 24.96 percent.

As an employer, Berkshire matches the Social Security and Medicare taxes paid by its employees. These taxes are borne by the shareholders of Berkshire for the same reasons corporate income taxes are. Using reasonable assumptions and data gleaned from the company's 2010 SEC filings, Buffett's share of these taxes was approximately $400 million in 2010. If these taxes are included (and they certainly should be), his 2010 "federal tax rate" increases by 6.16 percentage points to 31.12 percent.

Let's do the math. Buffett, in his analysis, overstated his office workers' "federal tax rate" by including irrelevant payroll taxes (7.65 percent) and employer-paid payroll taxes (7.65 percent). In actuality, his office workers' relevant 2010 "federal tax rate" was 20.7 percent, not 36.0 percent.

Buffett, in his analysis, ignored his share of corporate income taxes paid by the company he owns a third of. By doing so, he understated his "federal tax rate" by 7.56 percentage points. In addition, he ignored his share of Social Security and Medicare taxes paid by Berkshire. In doing so, he understated his "federal tax rate" by an additional 6.16 percentage points. If you're keeping score, Buffett's relevant 2010 "federal tax rate" was actually 31.12 percent, not 17.4 percent. Bottom line: Buffett's 2010 relevant "federal tax rate" was actually at least 10.4 percentage points higher than the average rate paid by his office workers.

Who knew?

It is quite troubling that Buffett's original *Times* op-ed piece, based upon such a flawed and very incomplete analysis, has gained such unchallenged visibility and credibility within the landscape of American politics. While Buffett should be chastised for putting out such an inaccurate and misleading analysis, political commentators on the right should be faulted for not doing their research and for not effectively raising a challenge against the flawed thinking underlying Buffett's op-ed.

(Editor's Note: This essay originally appeared in Forbes *in October, 2013.)*

SUMMARY

- Warren Buffett created a new tax metric by combining individual income taxes and payroll taxes into one "federal tax rate". He then asserted that his 2010 "federal tax rate" of 17.4 percent was 18.6 percentage points lower than the 36.0 percent average "federal tax rate" paid by his office workers
- The 2010 Social Security and Medicare taxing mechanisms in place in 2010 were inherently fair. Ascribing a "federal tax rate" differential to employee-paid payroll taxes, as Buffett did, is analytically incorrect. This 7.65 percentage point "federal tax rate" differential is a mirage

- Incredibly, Buffett included employer-paid (matching) payroll taxes into his calculations as well, thus doubling the 7.65 percentage point differential
- Buffett ignored, in his calculations, roughly $1.6 billion in corporate income taxes borne by him in 2010 as a one-third owner of Berkshire Hathaway. He also ignored his share (roughly $400 million) of Social Security and Medicare matching taxes paid by Berkshire Hathaway
- The analytically correct comparison, excluding individual payroll taxes and including corporate income and payroll taxes, shows that Buffett's "federal tax rate" was actually over 10 percentage points higher than the average rate of his office workers in 2010

45

"PROFIT IS EVIDENCE OF SUSPICIOUS BEHAVIOR"

By Lawrence W. Reed

A GREAT TRUTH IS ENCAPSULATED IN THIS COMMENT WIDELY ATTRIBUTED TO Samuel Gompers, "The worst crime against working people is a company which fails to operate at a profit."

Gompers was the founder of the American Federation of Labor. He appreciated something back then that many of today's progressives don't: *An economy without profit is an economy in deep, deep depression.*

Perhaps no progressive ever actually put it in the same terms as the title of this essay, but it's a fact that progressives routinely frown at the very mention of profit. To them, it's a dirty word (mainly if other people earn one, but not when they do).

Here's another related comment:

"The economic situation of enterprises will have to depend directly on profit, and profit cannot fulfill its function until prices are liberated from subsidies. Over the centuries, humankind has found no more effective measure of work than profit. Only profit can measure the quantity and quality of economic activity and permit us to relate production costs to results effectively and unambiguously.... Our suspicious attitude toward profit is a historical misunderstanding, the result of the economic illiteracy of people…"

Those words were written by economist Nikolaay Shmelyov in the June 1987 issue of *Novy Mir*, the leading political and literary journal of the then-Soviet Union, no less. The Soviets, after years of anti-profit propaganda and policies that produced a world-class basket case economy, were showing signs of shedding some of that economic illiteracy by the late 1980s.

The settlers at the Plymouth colony whose legendary feast led to the Thanksgiving holiday tradition nearly wiped themselves out when they set up a communal, socialistic economy. Each person was producing for everybody else and received an equal share of the total production. In the absence of a strong profit motive, the settlers starved until Gov. Bradford altered the arrangement. Thereafter, men and women produced for profit and the result was bountiful harvests with full Thanksgiving tables.

The people who don't like profit prefer to extol the virtue of selflessness, the charitable motive. A loving, caring concern for others can be a beautiful thing, especially when it's genuinely from the heart. Of their own free will, Americans have always been the most charitable, giving people on the planet. But the fact remains that profit is responsible for more good things—by a long shot—than all the charity in the world.

As you read this, gaze around the room in which you're seated. Notice the furniture, the building itself, your computer and smart phone, the clothing you're wearing. How much of what you see came into being because someone wanted to break even or lose money just to make you comfortable?

Consider this the next time you feast at the Thanksgiving table. The people who raised the turkey didn't do so because they wanted to help you out. The others who grew the cranberries and the yams didn't go to the trouble and expense out of some sacrificial or even charitable impulse. If you think those folks and the others who made almost everything else you own performed their tasks as sacrificial rituals, then you probably believe the old McDonald's slogan when they said in their commercials a while back, "We do it all for you."

Here's a simple, layman's way of viewing profit: Imagine you have a hundred dollars' worth of raw material. You shake it up, add your ingenuity and labor, and end up with a final product that people in the marketplace will pay $150 for. You've added value to society and earned a profit because of it. Now imagine that you take that same hundred dollars' worth of stuff, shake it up, and produce a final product worth only $50. You've certainly made no profit, and have actually subtracted from total value in society. How can that possibly be virtuous? And furthermore, which do you think is easier to accomplish year-after-year—a profit or a loss? I assure you that it takes no special skill or talent to consistently generate a loss. It's often tough just to break even.

Economists see profit in an even more insightful way. To them, profit is not some amorphous lump of what's left over after costs are paid. It's actually composed of several important components. In a typical small business in which the owner is also the manager, what he pays himself out of profit is "managerial remuneration." It may be small or nonexistent in the early, formative stages of the business but in most cases, it must ultimately be substantial enough to keep him from giving up and finding employment elsewhere. A second component of profit is interest on capital invested. Over the long run, any business must earn enough to pay a competitive return to its investors or they will take their capital someplace else.

If a business generates profit above and beyond what it takes to pay its owners, managers and investors a competitive return, then it has earned a third component that economists call "entrepreneurial profit" (sometimes called "economic profit"). When a particular business comes to market with a new or greatly improved product before anyone else thinks of it, meeting genuine needs and desires in ways that attract eager customers, the resulting "entrepreneurial profits" may at first be sizable. But the bigger they are, the more they attract additional supply (from the original provider as well as from competitors), and those high profits soon evaporate. In hindsight, it's apparent that the high profits acted as a signal to producers that declared, "Hey, look over here! People really want this thing, and more of it!"

Sometimes, people turn up their noses at a big firm that earns a bottom-line profit that sounds like a big number. "Walmart made an astonishing $16 billion in profit in 2014! Such greed! That's way too much!" These are the rants of the prejudiced and uninformed. Yes, Walmart profits in 2014 were about $16 billion. But they were earned on sales of $476 billion, resulting in profits as a percentage of sales of a mere 3.4 percent. The company paid *far* more in taxes and in wages than it earned in profits. Likewise, energy companies pay many times more in direct and hidden taxes on every gallon of gasoline, yet they are vilified for it while government, which took none of the risk and produced none of the product, rakes in its taxes and earns the praise of progressives for having done so.

In Marxist North Korea, there's a regime that works night and day to see that nobody makes a profit. There won't be anything like Thanksgiving dinner in North Korea this year, and that's no coincidence.

The hostility toward profit, whether motivated by envy or ignorance or demagoguery, is undeserved with this exception: when it's generated because of a firm's use of political connections to rig the market or attain subsidies and special favors from politicians at the expense of others. Otherwise, in free markets, it's more than just healthy—it's indispensable to the process of enhancing life and progress. It's what all of us seek when we try to improve our well-being by improving that of others through peaceful commerce.

Profit is not evidence of suspicious behavior, but raising fears and unfounded accusations against it certainly is.

SUMMARY

- Profit earned in free and competitive markets is the target of the misinformed and the uninformed; it's evidence of value added, not value subtracted
- Profit is a great motivator and incentivizer

- As most economists see it, profit is composed of managerial remunerations, interest on capital invested and "entrepreneurial" or "economic" profits
- By itself, the sheer dollar amount of a firm's profits tells you nothing about profit as a portion of sales or as a return on capital invested

46

"ROBOTS AND COMPUTERIZATION CAUSE UNEMPLOYMENT"

By Wendy R. McElroy

"REPORT SUGGESTS NEARLY HALF OF U.S. JOBS ARE VULNERABLE TO COMPUTER-ization," screams a headline. The cry of "robots are coming to take our jobs!" is ringing across North America. But the concern reveals nothing so much as a fear—and misunderstanding—of the free market.

In the short term, robotics will cause some job dislocation; in the long term, labor patterns will simply shift. The use of robotics to increase productivity while decreasing costs works basically the same way as past technological advances, like the production line, have worked. Those advances improved the quality of life of billions of people and created new forms of employment that were unimaginable at the time.

Given that reality, the cry that should be heard is, "Beware of monopolies controlling technology through restrictive patents or other government-granted privilege."

Actually, they are here already. Technological advance is an inherent aspect of a free market in which innovators seeks to produce more value at a lower cost. Entrepreneurs want a market edge. Computerization, industrial control systems, and robotics have become an integral part of that quest. Many manual jobs, such as factory-line assembly, have been phased out and replaced by others, such jobs related to technology, the Internet, and games. For a number of reasons, however, robots are poised to become villains of unemployment. Two reasons come to mind:

1. *Robots are now highly developed and less expensive.* Such traits make them an increasingly popular option. The *Banque de Luxembourg News* offered a snapshot:

   The currently-estimated average unit cost of around $50,000 should certainly decrease further with the arrival of "low-cost" robots on the market. This is particularly the case for "Baxter," the humanoid robot with evolving artificial intelligence from the U.S. company Rethink Robotics, or "Universal 5" from the Danish company Universal Robots, priced at just $22,000 and $34,000 respectively.

Better, faster, and cheaper are the bases of increased productivity.

2. *Robots will be interacting more directly with the general public.* The fast-food industry is a good example. People may be accustomed to ATMs, but a robotic kiosk that asks, "Do you want fries with that?" will occasion widespread public comment, albeit temporarily.

Comment from displaced fast-food restaurant workers may not be so transient. *NBC News* recently described a strike by workers in an estimated 150 cities. The workers' main demand was a $15 minimum wage, but they also called for better working conditions. The protesters, ironically, are speeding up their own unemployment by making themselves expensive and difficult to manage.

Compared to humans, robots are cheaper to employ—partly for natural reasons and partly because of government intervention.

Among the natural costs are training, safety needs, overtime, and personnel problems such as hiring, firing and on-the-job theft.

Now, according to *Singularity Hub*, robots can also be more productive in certain roles. They "can make a burger in 10 seconds (360/hr). Fast yes, but also superior quality. Because the restaurant is free to spend its savings on better ingredients, it can make gourmet burgers at fast food prices."

Government-imposed costs include minimum-wage laws and mandated benefits, as well as discrimination, liability, and other employment lawsuits. The employment advisory *Workforce* explained, "Defending a case through discovery and a ruling on a motion for summary judgment can cost an employer between $75,000 and $125,000. If an employer loses summary judgment—which, much more often than not, is the case—the employer can expect to spend a total of $175,000 to $250,000 to take a case to a jury verdict at trial."

At some point, human labor will make sense only to restaurants that wish to preserve the "personal touch" or to fill a niche.

The tech site *Motherboard* aptly commented, "The coming age of robot workers chiefly reflects a tension that's been around since the first common lands were enclosed by landowners who declared them private property: that between labour and the owners of capital. The future of labour in the robot age has everything to do with capitalism."

Ironically, *Motherboard* points to one critic of capitalism who defended technological advances in production: none other than Karl Marx. He called machines "fixed capital." The defense occurs in a segment called "The Fragment on Machines" in the unfinished but published manuscript *Grundrisse der Kritik der Politischen Ökonomie* (*Outlines of the Critique of Political Economy*).

Marx believed the "variable capital" (workers) dislocated by machines would be freed from the exploitation of their "surplus labor," the difference between their wages and the selling price of a product, which the capitalist pockets as profit. Machines would benefit "emancipated labour" because capitalists would "employ people upon something not directly and immediately productive, e.g. in the erection of machinery." The relationship change would revolutionize society and hasten the end of capitalism itself.

Never mind that the idea of "surplus labor" is intellectually bankrupt, technology ended up strengthening capitalism. But Marx was right about one thing: many workers have been emancipated from soul-deadening, repetitive labor. Many who feared technology did so because they viewed society as static. The free market is the opposite. It is a dynamic, quick-response ecosystem of value. Internet pioneer Vint Cerf argues, "Historically, technology has created more jobs than it destroys and there is no reason to think otherwise in this case."

Forbes pointed out that U.S. unemployment rates have changed little over the past 120 years (1890 to 2014) despite massive advances in workplace technology:

> There have been three major spikes in unemployment, all caused by financiers, not by engineers: the railroad and bank failures of the Panic of 1893, the bank failures of the Great Depression, and finally the Great Recession of our era, also stemming from bank failures. And each time, once the bankers and policymakers got their houses in order, businesses, engineers, and entrepreneurs restored growth and employment.

The drive to make society static is a powerful obstacle to that restored employment. How does society become static? A key word in the answer is "monopoly." But we should not equivocate on two forms of monopoly.

A monopoly established by aggressive innovation and excellence will dominate only as long as it produces better or less expensive goods than others can. Monopolies created by crony capitalism are entrenched expressions of privilege that serve elite interests. Crony capitalism is the economic arrangement by which business success depends upon having a close relationship with government, including legal privileges.

Restrictive patents are a basic building block of crony capitalism because they grant a business the "right" to exclude competition. Many libertarians deny the legitimacy of *any* patents. The nineteenth century classical liberal Eugen von Böhm-Bawerk rejected patents. He called them "legally compulsive relationships of patronage which are based on a vendor's exclusive right of sale": in short, a government-granted privilege that violated every man's right to compete freely. Modern critics of patents include the Austrian economist Murray Rothbard and intellectual property attorney Stephan Kinsella.

Pharmaceuticals and technology are particularly patent-hungry. The extent of the hunger can be gauged by how much money companies spend to protect their intellectual property rights. In 2011, Apple and Google reportedly spent more on patent lawsuits and purchases than on research and development. A *New York Times* article addressed the costs imposed on tech companies by "patent trolls"—people who do not produce or supply services based on patents they own but use them only to collect licensing fees and legal settlements. "Litigation costs in the United States related to patent assertion entities [trolls]," the article claimed, "totaled nearly $30 billion in 2011, more than four times the costs in 2005." These costs and associated ones, like patent infringement insurance, harm a society's productivity by creating stasis and preventing competition.

Dean Baker, co-director of the progressive Center for Economic Policy Research, described the difference between robots produced on the marketplace and robots produced by monopoly. Private producers "won't directly get rich" because "robots will presumably be relatively cheap to make. After all, we can have robots make them. If the owners of robots get really rich it will be because the government has given them patent monopolies so that they can collect lots of money from anyone who wants to buy or build a robot." The monopoly "tax" will be passed on to impoverish both consumers and employees.

Ultimately, we should return again to the wisdom of Joseph Schumpeter, who reminds us that technological progress, while it can change the patterns of production, tends to free up resources for new uses, making life better over the long term. In other words, the displacement of workers by robots is just creative destruction in action. Just as the car starter replaced the buggy whip, the robot might replace the burger-flipper. Perhaps the burger-flipper will migrate to a new profession, such as caring for an elderly person or cleaning homes for busy professionals. But there are always new ways to create value.

An increased use of robots will cause labor dislocation, which will be painful for many workers in the near term. But if market forces are allowed to function, the dislocation will be temporary. And if history is a guide, the replacement jobs will require skills that better express what it means to be human: communication, problem-solving, creation, and caregiving.

(Editor's Note: This essay first appeared in The Freeman *in September 2014 under the title, "Ludd vs Schumpeter.")*

SUMMARY

- The use of robotics to increase productivity while decreasing costs works basically the same way as past technological advances, like the production line, have worked. Those advances improved the quality of life of billions of people and created new forms of employment that were unimaginable at the time
- Compared to humans, robots are cheaper to employ—partly for natural reasons and partly because of government intervention. Natural costs include training, safety needs, overtime, and personnel problems such as hiring, firing and on-the-job theft. Unnatural, non-market costs stem from cronyism dispensed by governments
- An increased use of robots will cause labor dislocation, which will be painful for many workers in the near term. But if market forces are allowed to function, the dislocation will be temporary

47

"STATISTICAL DISPARITIES BETWEEN RACES PROVE DISCRIMINATION"

By Walter E. Williams

GEORGE ORWELL ADMONISHED, "SOMETIMES THE FIRST DUTY OF INTELLIGENT MEN is the restatement of the obvious." That's what I want to do—talk about the obvious.

Law professors, courts, and social scientists have long held that gross statistical disparities between races are evidence of a pattern and practice of discrimination. Behind this vision is the notion that but for discrimination, we'd be distributed proportionately by race across socioeconomic characteristics such as income, education, occupations, and other outcomes.

There is no evidence from anywhere on earth or any time in human history which demonstrates that but for discrimination there would be proportional representation and absence of gross statistical disparities by race, sex, nationality, or any other human characteristic. Nonetheless, much of our thinking, laws, litigation, and public policy are based on proportionality being the norm. Let us acknowledge a few gross disparities and decide whether they represent what lawyers and judges call a "pattern and practice of discrimination," while at the same time think-ing about what corrective action might be taken.

Jews are not even one percent of the world's population and only three percent of the U.S. population, but they are 20 percent of the world's Nobel Prize winners and 39 percent of American Nobel winners. That's a gross statistical disparity. Is the Nobel committee discriminating in favor of Jews, or are Jews engaging in an educational conspiracy against the rest of us? By the way, during Germany's Weimar Republic, Jews were only one percent of the German population, but they were ten percent of the country's doctors and dentists, 17 percent of its lawyers, and a large percentage of its scientific community. Jews won 27 percent of Nobel Prizes won by Germans.

The National Basketball Association in 2011 had nearly 80 percent black and 17 percent white players. But if that disparity is disconcerting, Asians are only one percent. Compounding this racial disparity, the highest-paid NBA players are black, and blacks have won Most Valuable Player 45 of the 57 times it has been awarded. Such a gross disparity works in reverse in the National Hockey League, where less than three percent of the players are black. Blacks are 66 percent of NFL and AFL professional football players. Among the 34 percent of other players, there's not a single Japanese player. But not to worry, according to the *Japan Times Online* (Jan. 17, 2012), "Dallas Cowboys scout Larry Dixon believes that as the world is getting smaller through globalization, there will one day be a Japanese player in the National Football League— though he can't guarantee when."

While black professional baseball players have fallen from 18 percent two decades ago to 8.8 percent today, there are gross disparities in achievement. Four out of the six highest career home-run totals were accumulated by black players, and each of the eight players who stole more than 100 bases in a season was black. Blacks who trace their ances-try to West Africa, including black Americans, hold more than 95 percent of the top times in sprinting.

How does one explain these gross sports disparities? Do they war-rant the attention of the courts?

There are some other disparities that might bother the diversity people. For example, Asians routinely get the highest scores on the math portion of the SAT, while blacks get the lowest.

Then there are deadly racial/ethnic disparities. Vietnamese American women have an incidence rate of cervical cancer that is five times higher than that of Caucasian women. The rates of liver cancer among Chinese, Filipino, Japanese, Korean, and Vietnamese populations are two to eleven times higher than that among Caucasians. Tay-Sachs disease is rare among populations other than Ashkenazi Jews (of European descent) and the Cajun population of southern Louisiana. The Pima Indians of Arizona have the highest known diabetes rates in the world. Prostate cancer is nearly twice as common among black men as it is among white men.

Then there's the issue of segregation. The *New York Times* "Room for Debate" section on May 21, 2012, led with, "Jim Crow is dead, segregation lives on. Is it time to bring back busing?" The Civil Rights Project of Harvard University in January 2003 declared that schools are racially segregated and becoming more so, adding, "Civil rights goals have not been accomplished. The country has been going backward toward greater segregation in all parts of the country for more than a decade." Six years later, the Civil Rights Project at UCLA reported that "schools in the United States are more segregated today than they have been in more than four decades."

Let's look at segregation. Casual observation of ice hockey games suggests that blacks' attendance is by no means proportional to their numbers in the general population. A similar observation can be made about black attendance at operas, dressage performances, and wine tastings. The population statistics of South Dakota, Iowa, Maine, Montana, Wyoming, and Vermont show that not even one percent of their populations are black. On the other hand, in states such as Georgia, Alabama, and Mississippi, blacks are overrepresented in terms of their percentage in the general population.

Blacks are a bit over 50 percent of the Washington, D.C., population. Reagan National Airport serves the Washington, D.C., area. Like other airports, it has water fountains. At no time has the writer observed anything close to blacks being 50 percent of water fountain users. It is a wild guess, but I speculate that on any day, not more than 10 or 15 percent of the people at water fountains are black. Would anyone suggest that Reagan National Airport water fountains are racially segregated? Would we declare South Dakota, Iowa, Maine, Montana, Wyoming, and Vermont racially segregated? Are ice hockey games, operas, dressage performances, and wine tastings racially segregated? Moreover, would anyone propose busing blacks to South Dakota, Iowa, Maine, Montana, and Wyoming and whites from those states to Georgia, Alabama, and Mississippi to achieve racial balance? What corrective action might be taken to achieve racial integration at ice hockey games, operas, dressage performances, and wine tastings?

A little reflection shows that people give the term "racial segregation" one meaning for water fountains, operas, and ice hockey games, and an entirely different meaning for schools. The sensible test to determine whether Reagan National Airport water fountains are segregated is to see whether a black is free to drink at any fountain. If the answer is affirmative, the fountains are not racially segregated even if no blacks drink at the fountains. The identical test should also be used for schools. Namely, if a black student lives within a particular school district, is he free to attend a particular school? If so, the school is not segregated, even if not a single black attends. When an activity is not racially mixed today, a better term is "racially homogeneous," which does not mean segregated in the historic usage of the term.

I hope that the people who say schools are segregated won't make the same claim about water fountains, states, operas, and ice hockey games.

(Editor's Note: This essay was originally published in November 2012 under the title, "Diversity, Ignorance and Stupidity" in The Freeman.*)*

SUMMARY

- There is no evidence from anywhere on earth or any time in human history which demonstrates that but for discrimination there would be proportional representation and absence of gross statistical disparities by race, sex, nationality, or any other human characteristic
- Casual observation of ice hockey games suggests that blacks' attendance is by no means proportional to their numbers in the general population but that's not evidence of "discrimination"

48

"THE SOLUTION TO OVER-POPULATION IS POPULATION CONTROL"

By Walter E. Williams

ACCORDING TO AN *AMERICAN DREAM* ARTICLE, "AL GORE, AGENDA 21 AND POPULATION Control," there are too many of us and it has a negative impact on the earth. Here's what the United Nations Population Fund said in its annual *State of the World Population Report* for 2009, "Facing a Changing World: Women, Population and Climate": "Each birth results not only in the emissions attributable to that person in his or her lifetime, but also the emissions of all his or her descendants. Hence, the emissions savings from intended or planned births multiply with time.... No human is genuinely 'carbon neutral,' especially when all greenhouse gases are figured into the equation. Therefore, everyone is part of the problem, so everyone must be part of the solution in some way.... Strong family planning programmes are in the interests of all countries for greenhouse-gas concerns as well as for broader welfare concerns."

Thomas Friedman agrees in his *New York Times* column "The Earth is Full" (June 8, 2008), in which he says, "[P]opulation growth and global warming push up food prices, which leads to political instability, which leads to higher oil prices, which leads to higher food prices, and so on in a vicious circle."

In his article "What Nobody Wants to Hear, But Everyone Needs to Know," University of Texas at Austin biology professor Eric R. Pianka wrote, "I do not bear any ill will toward people. However, I am convinced that the world, including all humanity, WOULD clearly be much better off without so many of us."

However, there is absolutely no relationship between high populations, disaster, and poverty. Population-control advocates might consider the Democratic Republic of Congo's meager 75 people per square mile to be ideal while Hong Kong's 6,500 people per square mile is problematic. Yet Hong Kong's citizens enjoy a per capita income of $43,000 while the Democratic Republic of Congo, one of the world's poorest countries, has a per capita income of $300. It's no anomaly. Some of the world's poorest countries have the lowest population densities.

Planet Earth is loaded with room. We could put the world's entire population into the United States, yielding a density of 1,713 people per square mile. That's far lower than what now exists in all major U.S. cities. The entire U.S. population could move to Texas, and each family of four would enjoy more than 2.1 acres of land. Likewise, if the entire world's population moved to Texas, California, Colorado, and Pennsylvania, each family of four would enjoy a bit over two acres. Nobody's suggesting that the entire earth's population be put in the United States or that the entire U.S. population move to Texas. I cite these figures to help put the matter into perspective.

Let's look at some other population density evidence. Before the collapse of the Soviet Union, West Germany had a higher population density than East Germany. The same is true of South Korea versus North Korea; Taiwan, Hong Kong, and Singapore versus China; the United States versus the Soviet Union; and Japan versus India. Despite more crowding, West Germany, South Korea, Taiwan, Hong Kong, Singapore, the United States, and Japan experienced far greater economic growth, higher standards of living, and greater access to resources than their counterparts with lower population densities. By the way, Hong Kong has virtually no agriculture sector, but its citizens eat well.

One wonders why anyone listens to doomsayers who have been consistently wrong in their predictions—not a little off, but way off. Professor Paul Ehrlich, author of the 1968 bestseller *The Population Bomb*, predicted major food shortages in the United States and that by "the 1970s...hundreds of millions of people are going to starve to death." Ehrlich forecasted the starvation of 65 million Americans between 1980 and 1989 and a decline in U.S. population to 22.6 million by 1999. He saw England in more desperate straits: "If I were a gambler, I would take even money that England will not exist in the year 2000."

By a considerable measure, poverty in underdeveloped nations is directly attributable to their leaders heeding the advice of western "experts." Nobel laureate and Swedish economist Gunnar Myrdal said (1956), "The special advisors to underdeveloped countries who have taken the time and trouble to acquaint themselves with the problem...all recommend central planning as the first condition of progress." In 1957 Stanford University economist Paul A. Baran advised, "The establishment of a socialist planned economy is an essential, indeed indispensable, condition for the attainment of economic and social progress in underdeveloped countries."

Topping off this bad advice, underdeveloped countries sent their brightest to the London School of Economics, Berkeley, Harvard, and Yale to be taught socialist nonsense about economic growth. Nobel laureate economist Paul Samuelson taught them that underdeveloped countries "cannot get their heads above water because their production is so low that they can spare nothing for capital formation by which the standard of living could be raised." Economist Ranger Nurkse describes the "vicious circle of poverty" as the basic cause of the underdevelopment of poor countries. According to him, a country is poor because it is poor. On its face this theory is ludicrous. If it had validity, all mankind would still be cave dwellers because we all were poor at one time and poverty is inescapable.

Population controllers have a Malthusian vision of the world that sees population growth outpacing the means for people to care for themselves. Mankind's ingenuity has proven the Malthusians dead wrong. As a result we can grow increasingly larger quantities of food on less and less land. The energy used to produce food, per dollar of GDP, has been in steep decline. We're getting more with less, and that applies to most other inputs we use for goods and services.

Ponder the following question: Why is it that mankind today enjoys cell phones, computers, and airplanes but did not when King Louis XIV was alive? After all, the necessary physical resources to make cell phones, computers, and airplanes have always been around, even when cavemen walked the earth. There is only one reason we enjoy these goodies today but did not in past eras. It's the growth in human knowledge, ingenuity, and specialization and trade—coupled with personal liberty and private property rights—that led to industrialization and betterment. In other words human beings are immensely valuable resources.

What are called overpopulation problems result from socialistic government practices that reduce the capacity of people to educate, clothe, house, and feed themselves. Underdeveloped nations are rife with farm controls, export and import restrictions, restrictive licensing, price controls, plus gross human rights violations that encourage their most productive people to emigrate and stifle the productivity of those who remain. The true antipoverty lesson for poor nations is that the most promising route out of poverty to greater wealth is personal liberty and its main ingredient, limited government.

(Editor's Note: This essay was originally published in November 2011 under the title, "Population Control Nonsense" in The Freeman.*)*

SUMMARY

- There is no relationship between high populations, disaster, and poverty

- By a considerable measure, poverty in underdeveloped nations is directly attributable to their leaders heeding the advice of western "experts" who champion repressive, redistributive and anti-private property "solutions"
- What are called overpopulation problems result from socialistic government practices that reduce the capacity of people to educate, clothe, house, and feed themselves

49

"RESOURCE-POOR COUNTRIES NEED STRONG CENTRAL PLANNING TO DEVELOP"

By Lawrence W. Reed

Countries are well cultivated, not as they are fertile,
but as they are free.

—*Charles de Montesquieu*

THREE CHEERS FOR HONG KONG, THAT TINY CHUNK OF SOUTHEAST ASIAN ROCK.
For the twentieth consecutive year, the Index of Economic Freedom—
compiled by the *Wall Street Journal* and the Heritage Foundation—
ranks Hong Kong (HK) as the freest economy in the world. Its success
is an intellectual embarrassment to the progressive ideology.

Though part of mainland China since the British ceded it in 1997,
HK is governed locally on a daily basis. So far, the Chinese have remained
reasonably faithful to their promise to leave the HK economy alone.
What makes it so free is music to the ears of everyone who loves liberty:
Relatively little corruption. An efficient and independent judiciary.
Respect for the rule of law and property rights. An uncomplicated tax
system with low rates on both individuals and business and an overall
tax burden that's a mere 14 percent of GDP (half the U.S. rate). No taxes
on capital gains or interest income or even on earnings from outside of

HK. No sales tax or VAT either. A very light regulatory touch. No government budget deficit and almost nonexistent public debt. Oh, and don't forget its average tariff rate of near zero. That's right—*zero*!

This latest ranking in the *WSJ*/Heritage report confirms what Canada's Fraser Institute found in its latest Economic Freedom of the World Index, which also ranked HK as the world's freest. The World Bank rates the "ease of doing business" in HK as just about the best on the planet.

To say that an economy is "the freest" is to say that it's "the most capitalist." Capitalism is what happens when you leave peaceful people alone. It doesn't require some elaborate and artificial, Rube Goldberg contrivance cooked up by tenured central planners in their insular ivory towers. But if we are to believe the critics of capitalism, HK must also be a veritable Hell's Kitchen of greed, poverty, exploitation and despair.

Not so. Not even close.

Maybe this is why progressives don't like to talk about Hong Kong: It's not only the freest economy, it's also one of the richest. Its per capita income, at 264 percent of the world's average, has more than doubled in the past 15 years. People don't flee from HK; they flock to it. At the close of World War II, the population numbered 750,000. Today it's nearly ten times that, at 7.1 million.

The news that the HK economy is once again rated the world's freest is an occasion to celebrate the one man most responsible for this perennial achievement. The name of Sir John James Cowperthwaite (1915–2006) should forever occupy top shelf in the pantheon of great people. Some of us just write about ideas of liberty and free enterprise. This guy actually made them public policy for millions of citizens.

The late Milton Friedman explained in a 1997 tribute to Cowperthwaite how remarkable his economic legacy is: "Compare Britain—the birthplace of the Industrial Revolution, the nineteenth-century economic superpower on whose empire the sun never set—with Hong Kong, a spit of land, overcrowded, with no resources except for a great harbor. Yet within four decades the residents of this spit of overcrowded land had achieved a level of income one-third higher than that enjoyed by the residents of its former mother country."

A Scot by birth, Cowperthwaite attended Merchiston Castle School in Edinburgh and then studied classics at St. Andrews University and at Christ's College at Cambridge. He served in the British Colonial Administrative Service in HK during the early 1940s. After the war he was asked to come up with plans for the government to boost economic growth. To his credit, he had his eyes open and noticed that the economy was already recovering quite nicely without government direction. So while the mother country lurched in a socialist direction at home under Clement Attlee, Cowperthwaite became an advocate of what he called "positive non-interventionism" in HK. Later as the colony's Financial Secretary from 1961 to 1971, he personally administered it.

"Over a wide field of our economy it is still the better course to rely on the nineteenth century's 'hidden hand' than to thrust clumsy bureaucratic fingers into its sensitive mechanism," Cowperthwaite declared in 1962. "In particular, we cannot afford to damage its mainspring, freedom of competitive enterprise." He didn't like protectionism or subsidies even for new, so-called "infant" industries: "An infant industry, if coddled, tends to remain an infant industry and never grows up or expands." He believed firmly that "in the long run, the aggregate of the decisions of individual businessmen, exercising individual judgment in a free economy, even if often mistaken, is likely to do less harm than the centralized decisions of a government; and certainly the harm is likely to be counteracted faster."

Ever since the days of John Maynard Keynes, economics has been cursed by the notion that human action should be distilled into numbers, which then become a "pretense to knowledge" for central planner types. In many collegiate economics courses, it's hard to tell where the math leaves off and the actual economics begins. To Cowperthwaite, the planner's quest for statistics was anathema. So he refused to compile them. When Friedman asked him in 1963 about the "paucity of statistics," Cowperthwaite answered, "If I let them compute those statistics, they'll want to use them for planning."

If that sounds quaintly backward or archaic, let me remind you that the biggest economic flops of the past century were both centrally planned and infatuated with numbers. Whole ministries were devoted to their compilation because even lousy numbers gave the planners the illusion of control. But not in Hong Kong!

Statistics, no matter how accurate or voluminous, are no substitute for sound principles. Powered by an abundance of the latter under Cowperthwaite, the HK economy soared during his tenure. Writing in the November 2008 issue of *The Freeman*, Andrew P. Morriss noted that in his decade as financial secretary, "real wages rose by 50 percent and the portion of the population in acute poverty fell from 50 to 15 percent." It's hard to argue with success. After Cowperthwaite's retirement in 1971, less principled successors dabbled in social welfare spending but they financed it through land sales, not increased taxation. Tax rates to this day are right where the old man left them.

(Editor's Note: The original version of this essay appeared in FEE's magazine, The Freeman, *under the title, "The Man Behind the Hong Kong Miracle" in February 2014).*

SUMMARY

- Hong Kong, a small rock with little resources but still a lot of economic freedom, shows that freedom goes a long way to ensuring progress no matter how few your resources are
- The biggest economic flops of the past century were both centrally planned and infatuated with numbers—in spite of being resource-rich

50

"PEOPLE LOVE THE ROBIN HOOD STORY BECAUSE HE TOOK FROM THE RICH TO GIVE TO THE POOR"

By B. K. Marcus

We are the sons of these serfs, of these tributaries, of these bourgeois that the conquerors devoured at will; we owe them all that we are.

—Augustin Thierry

A CARRIAGE IS BROUGHT TO A HALT ON THE ROAD TO NOTTINGHAM. THE NOBLES within peek past the curtains to see bandits on all sides. They scan the grimy faces of the hostile woodsman to see if they can recognize that famous outlaw, that protector and avenger of the poor and downtrodden, that paragon of armed social justice, that singular personification of class conflict: Robin Hood.

Generations have grown up with a heroic ideal of robbing from the rich and giving to the poor. Robin Hood's hawk-eyed archery and fierce swordplay make him popular with kids, and his social conscience endears him to their parents.

Only those who are particularly wary of an apparently "progressive" message in the legend take exception. Socialists, of course, make the most of Robin Hood as a hero of the underclass and a medieval precursor to modern Marxist class theory.

Because Robin Hood is a centuries-old folk hero and not a historical figure, each generation has been able to reinterpret the legend to fit its agenda. It was only in the nineteenth century, for example, that Robin Hood amended his modus operandi to include giving to the poor. But if we look to the era in which his legend first "became genuinely popular," according to historian Simon Schama, we'll see that the classes in conflict don't neatly fit the Marxist theory. They do, however, fit the older, now mostly forgotten libertarian class theory of French and American classical liberals.

Robin Hood's story is now commonly set in the late 1100s while King Richard the Lionheart is away, fighting in the Crusades, but our earliest written record of the legend appears some 200 years later, at a time of drastic changes in the lives of both rich and poor—and in the relationship between the two.

The Black Death reached English shores in 1348, killing almost half the population by 1350. The survivors were, of course, devastated. Not only had they lost their friends and families; they lost any sense of order in the world. The Middle Ages were marked by a belief in permanence and predictability. For the commoners who made up more than 90 percent of the English population, the details of one's life would have resembled those of one's grandparents and could be expected to be the same for one's grandchildren. Then everything changed.

The population became drastically smaller—especially among working people—but there was just as much gold, as many acres of farmland, and as many buildings and other artifacts of pre-plague England. There was, in short, the same amount of wealth in pre- and post-plague England, and only half as many people to possess it.

With fewer peasants to till the soil, landlords had to compete to attract the surviving labor. After many generations on the same few acres of land, healthy field workers were suddenly uprooting and moving to wherever they found the best opportunity. Market forces made the lives of working people immeasurably better—and the nobles who lost the bidding wars for their services didn't like it.

As happens in every era of dramatic change, the economic has-beens appealed to the coercive power of the State to return conditions to a comfortable status quo ante.

The Statute of Labourers (1351) made it illegal for peasants to accept wages that were higher than pre-plague levels. Meanwhile, food prices skyrocketed, as we should expect from a doubling of the supply of money relative to food supply.

The poor, forced to endure hunger and shortages, could see ever more clearly that the source of their suffering was not just bad weather or pestilence; it was a political class growing rich from peasant labor.

And if the Black Death had destroyed the survivors' belief in the security of an unchanging life, it also led them to question the supporting ideology of feudalism. The doctrine of the Great Chain of Being, which gave divine sanction to the aristocracy's superior position in society and in the economy, suddenly seemed as uncertain as everything else.

An oppressed people with a clear enemy and a belief in the reality of change is a recipe for revolution.

In 1381, in response to a new poll tax to pay for foreign war, thousands of commoners took up arms and advanced on London. The uprising is remembered as the English Peasants' Revolt, but as Schama notes in *A History of Britain*, "The 'Peasants' Revolt' of 1381 was, in fact, conspicuous for the absence of peasants."

The rank and file may have come from the bottom of the social hierarchy, but the leaders of the revolt were merchants and lawyers:

> the sort of people, in fact, who...had a bit of money and sometimes even a smattering of book learning. Their trades put them in touch with worlds beyond their parish, and they knew how to make an army out of those one rung down on the social ladder. (*A History of Britain*, vol. 1, p. 246)

In the BBC documentary version of his book, Schama asks and answers a key question for our understanding of the era and culture that produced the legend of Robin Hood:

> Was this a class war, then (a phrase we're not supposed to use since the official burial of Marxism)? Yes, it was.

But was it really? Schama makes it clear that the class theory he has in mind is Marxist, and Marx makes clear that the inescapable root conflict is between socioeconomic classes—specifically between rich and poor—no matter what system led to the creation and distribution of wealth.

The Communist Manifesto opens with these lines:

> The history of all hitherto existing society is the history of class struggles. Freeman and slave, patrician and plebeian, lord and serf, guild-master and journeyman, in a word, oppressor and oppressed....

In "Classical Liberal Roots of the Marxist Doctrine of Classes," historian Ralph Raico writes, "On examination these opposed pairs turn out to be, either wholly or in part, not economic, but legal, categories." (That is, categories created by *political* privilege.)

Not only can we see that that the Peasants' Revolt was a battle between the productive class of commoners and the specifically political class that fed off their production; this division of sides was also clear to the rebels themselves:

"They were emphatically not a rabble," writes Schama:

> En route [to London], their targets had been carefully selected: estates belonging to tax collectors or prominent members of the royal council. ... Any document bearing the green wax seal of the Exchequer was marked for destruction. It was an army that knew what it was doing.

If the Peasant's Revolt had been a class war in the Marxist sense, we would have seen the so-called peasants targeting wealth in general. Instead, we see a rebellion led by an emerging bourgeoisie targeting the machinery of the oppressive State.

Marx was not, however, the originator of class theory, and his is not the only version of class war that can describe the events of 1381. As he wrote in a letter, "Long before me bourgeois historians had described the historical development of this class struggle and bourgeois economists the economic anatomy of the classes."

The "bourgeois historians" were French and American classical liberals: Charles Comte, Charles Dunoyer, Augustin Thierry, and other disciples of Jean-Baptiste Say in France, and John Taylor of Caroline, William Leggett, John C. Calhoun, and other Jeffersonians in the United States. And their theory, unlike Marx's revision, divided the people into a productive economic class and a parasitic political class: tax payers and tax consumers. Historically, these classes correlated (not coincidentally) to the oppressed poor and the oppressive rich, but the liberal class theory did not treat the distribution of wealth as the *source* of inevitable conflict; the historical division of the rich and poor was in fact a result of the political class's coercive exploitation of productive people pursuing voluntary exchange in a free market.

We advocates of such voluntary exchange too often resist Robin Hood's rob-from-the-rich morality, as we resist any talk of fundamental conflicts of interest between different classes. But the targets of Robin Hood and his merry men—like the targets of the Peasants' Revolt—were rich from plunder, not production.

Like the radical liberals of the nineteenth century, the "peasant" rebels of the 1300s—when Robin Hood's exploits fired the imagination of an oppressed people—recognized that their enemies were the tax collectors, legislators, and all other members of the political class.

Our intellectual tradition not only offers an older, sounder class theory with greater explanatory power than the now more familiar Marxist theory; it lets us join the English rebels in embracing Robin Hood as a hero of the productive class.

(Editor's Note: The original version of this essay appeared in The Freeman *in June 2014.)*

SUMMARY

- Generations have grown up with a heroic ideal of Robin Hood robbing from the rich and giving to the poor but it was only in the 19th Century that he amended his modus operandi to include giving to the poor.
- Market forces emerging with the breakdown of feudalism in the late Middle Ages made the lives of working people immeasurably better—and the nobles who lost the bidding wars for their services didn't like it
- The targets of Robin Hood and his merry men were rich from plunder, not production

51

"GREEDY CAPITALISTS TAKE ADVANTAGE OF PEOPLE IN NATURAL DISASTERS; PRICE CONTROLS ARE THE ANSWER"

By Donald J. Boudreaux

THE IMMEDIATE AFTERMATH OF A NATURAL DISASTER INEVITABLY BRINGS MUCH higher prices for staple goods, such as lumber, batteries, fuel, and bottled water. Just as inevitably, these higher prices are roundly decried as unjust and inexcusable.

Such price hikes are slapped with the derisive name "price gouging." And even people who typically endorse markets often call for it to be outlawed. A recent example comes from *Times of India* columnist Swaminathan Aiyar, who describes himself as a market liberal. In his January 9, 2005 column, Aiyar condemned the price hikes that followed the devastating 2004 Asian tsunamis, referring to them as an additional tragedy visited upon already-suffering victims.

This interpretation of the price hikes is as unfortunate as it is mistaken. Let's review here some basic economics of "price gouging." Prices are not set arbitrarily. They are what they are for a variety of reasons. These reasons are summarized by the two words "supply" and "demand." Prices reflect existing conditions of supply and demand. If the price of bottled water rises, it does so either because supplies have fallen or because people's demand has risen. In the wake of natural disasters, both of these effects kick in strongly.

A natural disaster destroys inventories, vehicles, and infrastructure (including water-treatment plants and roads). Existing stocks of bottled water and of close substitutes, such as tap water, are reduced. Also reduced is the flow of supplies of water. Many of the roads and vehicles ordinarily used to carry bottled water to market are now destroyed. Less bottled water makes it to market in the devastated region. In short, supply falls significantly.

At the same time, demand for bottled water rises, principally because tap water is now less available and more dangerous. This fall in supply combined with rise in demand means that the value of each available bottle of water rises. People are willing to pay more for each bottle.

The higher price per bottle reflects the underlying reality; it reflects the fact that bottled-water supply is lower and bottled-water demand is higher. In short, it reflects the fact that bottled water is now more valuable than it was before the disaster.

Therefore, the fact that is unfortunate is not the higher price; it's the underlying reality reflected by the higher price. That a natural disaster destroyed supplies and supply lines is indeed unfortunate. But this is the reality. Because, as economist Thomas Sowell reminds us, reality is not optional so we ought to deal with it as best as we can.

And how best to deal with this unfortunate reality? To begin, never pretend that reality is other than what it is. Face reality squarely, fully, and soberly. If this advice sounds trite, understand that government-imposed prohibitions on "price gouging" mask the underlying reality, shielding people from the truth of it.

If the market value of a bottle of water is $25, preventing merchants from charging a price higher than $5 shields consumers from the fact that potable water is now more precious than it was pre-disaster. The price cap also shields suppliers from this same truth. The inevitable consequences of this hoax only add to the problems caused by the natural disaster. With the price artificially kept low—at its pre-disaster level—

consumers will try to use this now-more-precious commodity today with no more care than they used it yesterday.

But they can only try, for they'll not succeed in using bottled water with the same nonchalance as they did pre-disaster. Misled by the counterfeit low price, consumers initially will do nothing to use water more carefully. But as fast as you can say "tsunami," other signals will alert them to water's now-greater preciousness. Long queues to buy water will emerge, as will empty shelves, black markets, and reports of neighbors hoarding bottled water in their basements.

Not only will most people who want bottled water be unable to buy all they want at the counterfeit price, many will spend valuable time waiting in queues (often to no avail). Some will drive over obstructed roads to buy water in distant towns, while others will use their personal or political connections to obtain water.

Time and resources that could be better spent cleaning up and launching the rebuilding effort are diverted to frequently futile efforts to obtain bottled water. These consequences are avoidable misfortunes compounding the pain of the natural disaster. Note several regrettable facts.

Fact one: capping the price does not keep the cost of bottled water low. Time spent waiting, time and fuel spent driving to distant towns where supplies are greater, and the anxiety unleashed by the inability to obtain water are all costs. The fact that these costs are not revealed in the price of bottled water does not render them less significant or real.

Fact two: while a higher market price both prompts consumers *voluntarily* to economize more diligently on water's use and increases the quantity of water supplied (by giving incentives to suppliers to bring more water to this market), the queues and empty shelves generated by the price cap force consumers to economize, but do nothing to inspire suppliers to bring more water to market.

Fact three: the economization forced on consumers by price caps is ugly and arbitrary. Those obliged to do without are the unlucky ones who couldn't get into the queue early enough and who have no political or business connections. These unlucky consumers are also typically too poor to pay the high prices demanded on the black market. A fact always missed by proponents of price caps is that black-market prices are higher than the unregulated market prices would be. The reason is that unregulated market prices—being visible and legal—will stimulate a larger inflow of supplies than will black-market prices.

There's no denying that people dislike the higher prices. What is deniable is that the higher prices are the problem. They are not the problem; they reflect the problem. Because the problem itself is unfortunate, its undistorted reflection will reveal this misfortune. But only by revealing this misfortune as accurately as possible to everyone who can help to minimize its effects will reality be returned as quickly as possible to normal.

Still, why must merchants profit from other people's misfortune? Surely sellers can and should choose to sell their inventories at pre-disaster prices? Such questions reveal a deep and persistent objection to post-disaster price hikes—namely, it's simply unfair for merchants to profit from disasters.

Of course, merchants can voluntarily keep their prices below market levels. But to do so would be not only harmful but also unfair! If a grocer refuses to raise the price he charges for bottled water up to the market level, he will find his store besieged by consumers. Only consumers near the front of the line will be lucky enough to get the water; those closer to the rear will go home empty-handed. Is queuing a fair means of deciding who gets the water?

Also, by not raising the price, the grocer will mute the price signal sent to the global market that bottled water is especially needed in this locale. Muting this signal will reduce how much or the speed with which additional, much-needed supplies of bottled water are shipped from where they are valued less to the disaster area where they are desired more.

A better way for the merchant to extend a helping hand would be to charge market prices and, out of the profits he earns, to make cash contributions to cash-strapped victims of the disaster. Those contributions will enable victims to better express on the market their need for bottled water and other supplies—thus communicating to suppliers worldwide just how desperately they need things to help rebuild their lives—without diluting the incentives of all consumers to economize on the now-much-scarcer goods or the incentives of suppliers to turn their supplies to where they are now needed most urgently.

Thwarting market forces only worsens calamities and is therefore most unfair.

(Editor's Note: The original version of this essay was published by FEE in its magazine, The Freeman, *in April 2005 under the title, "On Price Gouging.")*

SUMMARY

- Prices are not set arbitrarily. They are what they are for a variety of reasons. These reasons are summarized by the two words "supply" and "demand"
- Government-imposed prohibitions on "price gouging" mask the underlying reality, shielding people from the truth of it
- Higher prices in the wake of reduced supplies result in conservation of what remains and the encouragement of new supplies, precisely what the situation calls for

52

"PROGRESSIVES HAVE GOOD INTENTIONS, SO WHAT ELSE IS REQUIRED?"

By Lawrence W. Reed

IS IT TOO MUCH TO ASK OF GOVERNMENT THAT IT DO A SMALL JOB RIGHT BEFORE it takes on a much bigger one?

If you're wearing the sight-proof blindfolds that most progressives wear, the answer is probably "YES."

Progressives advocate for a welfare state and sell it not so much on its track record (that would be embarrassing) but more for its good intentions. "We want to help people!" they exclaim. Definitions of the welfare state abound, and often depend on one's perspective. Here's my own brutally candid assessment:

> Since people are not decent and compassionate enough to assist their deserving fellows in distress, we must expect them to somehow elect politicians who are more decent and compassionate than they are. Those politicians will then take money from them under threat of imprisonment, launder it through an expensive bureaucracy, and spend what's left not

to actually solve the problem but to manage it into perpetuity for endless dependency, demagoguery and political gain. And then the advocates of the welfare state will pat themselves on the back and salve their guilty consciences. They will compliment themselves for possessing a monopoly on compassion and ignore the destructive results of their handiwork, except to condemn as "heartless" those with the audacity to point them out.

Take the federal Department of Veterans Affairs (*please!*). Its website says its primary job is to provide "patient care and federal benefits to veterans and their dependents." It manages more than a thousand hospitals, nursing facilities and health clinics. Horror stories emanating from this socialized medicine sampler are numerous and legendary. They include long waiting lists, staff shortages, death rates that would be unacceptable anywhere else in the country and care so shoddy that many veterans prefer to pay for private alternatives. But that doesn't stop progressives from plowing full steam ahead for even more government in health care.

Writing in the February 25, 2014 *Washington Examiner,* Mark Flatten provided the latest shocking revelation: To cover up its massive backlog of orders for medical services, the VA simply cancelled tens of thousands of scheduled exams and appointments. Voila! Get rid of the patients and you get rid of the embarrassing backlogs. Imagine the huge outcry if a private provider behaved this way. Would anyone in his right mind say, "Give that outfit some more patients and money!"?

But don't expect any scandal coming out of the VA to give pause to the progressive apologists for ever more government in health care. Being a progressive means never having to say you're sorry. Good intentions trump everything else. Apparently, the one thing progressives share with almost everyone else is a very *high* level of expectations for the private sector and a very *low* one for the public sector.

This raises a much more fundamental question about the progressive, big government folks: what's up with their thought process? It's so riddled with inconsistencies, non-sequiturs and dubious notions that the rest of us are often left scratching our heads in disbelief. Faulty, illogical or contradictory premises just might be the reason they often come to the wrong conclusions.

Over the years, I've observed quite a few attributes of the progressive thought process that are, to be polite, rather questionable. Here's a short list:

1. They spend more time promoting dependency than they do encouraging self-reliance.
2. Deceptions (for example, Barack Obama's "If you like your health care plan, you can keep your health care plan") don't rankle most of them because they believe their ends justify almost any means.
3. They think intentions matter far more than actual results.
4. They lump people into groups and assign them fictitious rights.
5. They learn little or nothing from history or economics.
6. They think emotions, slogans and bumper-stickers trump reason and logic.
7. Compassion is their favorite word even as they put a gun to your head.
8. They respect property if it's theirs, but not if it's yours.
9. They'd rather shut you up than engage you in serious debate.
10. Individuals are never among the minorities they say they support.
11. When the first conservative or libertarian faculty member is hired at their university, they think it's a hostile takeover.
12. They think a welfare check is an entitlement, but a paycheck isn't.
13. When their policies flop, they assume no responsibility and demand more of the same.
14. They're always busy reforming you even if their own lives are dysfunctional.

15. They claim to know the future (e.g., which industry to subsidize) while showing no evidence they even understand the past.

16. They dislike business less because they have sound arguments against it and more because they have no idea how to start or run one themselves.

17. They criticize people and companies for not paying more in taxes than they are legally required to, yet never make any "donations" to government themselves beyond their own legal tax liability.

18. They are angry most of the time, have no sense of humor, find victims under every bed, and can't even tell a joke that's reasonably funny.

19. They've perfected the fine art of the double-standard, exempting their own from the very actions they criticize in others.

20. They appeal to the worst in us by emphasizing racial divisions, pitting class against class, and buying votes with other people's money.

In *The Art of War*, Sun Tzu advised, "Know your enemy and know yourself and you can fight a hundred battles without disaster." Perhaps so, but it sure seems that the more you know about government-worshiping progressives, the harder it is to actually figure them out.

When it comes to the good intentions that progressives insist they possess, I'm willing to grant that most of them do indeed possess them. But it's preposterous to assume that those who oppose their proposals do *not* have good intentions. Moreover, it's wise to remember, as the old saying admonishes, that "The road to Hell is paved with good intentions."

Good intentions are not enough. Nowhere near enough, in fact. Other things matter too, such as reason, logic, moral principles, evidence, outcomes, history and experience, reality and facts.

(Editor's Note: A shorter version of this essay was first published under a different title at www.cnsnews.com.)

SUMMARY

- One thing progressives share with almost everyone else is a very *high* level of expectations for the private sector and a very *low* one for the public sector
- Good intentions are, by themselves, nowhere near enough

ABOUT THE EDITOR AND CO-AUTHOR

LAWRENCE W. ("LARRY") REED BECAME PRESIDENT OF THE FOUNDATION FOR Economic Education (FEE) in 2008, after serving as chairman of its board of trustees in the 1990s and both writing and speaking for FEE since the late 1970s. Prior to becoming FEE's president, he served for more than twenty years as president of the Mackinac Center for Public Policy in Midland, Michigan. He also taught Economics full-time from 1977 to 1984 at Northwood University in Michigan and chaired its Department of Economics from 1982 to 1984.

He holds a B.A. degree in Economics from Grove City College (1975) and an M.A. degree in History from Slippery Rock State University (1978), both in Pennsylvania. He holds two honorary doctorates, one from Central Michigan University (Public Administration—1993) and Northwood University (Laws—2008).

A champion for liberty, Reed has authored over 1,000 newspaper columns and articles, dozens of articles in magazines and journals in the U. S. and abroad. His writings have appeared in the *Wall Street Journal,*

Christian Science Monitor, USA Today, Baltimore Sun, Detroit News, and *Detroit Free Press*, among many others. He has authored or co-authored seven books, including *A Republic—If We Can Keep It, Striking the Root: Essays on Liberty, The Great Hope,* and *Are We Good Enough For Liberty?* He is frequently interviewed on radio talk shows and has appeared as a guest on numerous television programs, including those anchored by Judge Andrew Napolitano and John Stossel on Fox Business News.

Reed has delivered at least 75 speeches annually in the past 30 years—in virtually every state and dozens of countries from Bulgaria to China to Bolivia. His best-known lectures include "Seven Principles of Sound Policy" and "Great Myths of the Great Depression"—both of which have been translated into more than a dozen languages and distributed worldwide.

His interests in political and economic affairs have taken him as a freelance journalist to 81 countries on six continents since 1985. He is a member of the prestigious Mont Pelerin Society and an advisor to numerous organizations around the world. He served for 15 years as a member of the board (and one term as president) of the State Policy Network. His numerous recognitions include the "Champion of Freedom" award from the Mackinac Center for Public Policy and the "Distinguished Alumni" award from Grove City College.

He is a native of Pennsylvania and a 30-year resident of Michigan, and now resides in Newnan, Georgia.

CONTRIBUTING AUTHORS

Julian Adorney is an economic historian, entrepreneur, and fiction writer.

Charles W. Baird is a former Professor of Economics at California State University at East Bay, and a contributor to *The Freeman*.

Melvin D. Barger is a retired corporate public relations representative and writer who lives in Toledo, Ohio. He is a contributor for the Foundation for Economic Education's 1994 edition of the book, *Clichés of Politics*, edited by former FEE trustee Mark Spangler.

Max Borders is editor of *The Freeman* and director of content at the Foundation for Economic Education.

Donald J. Boudreaux is a past president of the Foundation for Economic Education and a Professor of Economics at George Mason University in Fairfax, Virginia.

Anne Rathbone Bradley is the Vice President of Economic Initiatives at the Institute for Faith, Work & Economics (IFWE), where she develops and commissions research toward a systematic biblical theology of economic freedom. A frequent lecturer at FEE seminars, she is a visiting professor at Georgetown University, and she also teaches at The Institute for World Politics and George Mason University. Additionally, she is a visiting scholar at the Bernard Center for Women, Politics, and Public Policy. She is an editor of and contributing author to IFWE's recently released book, *For the Least of These: A Biblical Answer to Poverty*.

Burton W. Folsom is a professor of history at Hillsdale College and authored Young America's Foundation's book, *The Myth of the Robber Barons*. Dr. Folsom is also the author of several bestselling books including *New Deal or Raw Deal: How FDR's Economic Legacy Has Damaged America*. In addition, along with his wife, Anita, he wrote the 2013 book, *FDR Goes to War*.

Gary M. Galles is Professor of Economics at Pepperdine University in Malibu, California.

George P. Harbison is a financial officer with an Atlanta, Georgia-based corporation.

Henry Hazlitt was a remarkable economist and journalist whose writings appeared widely during his lifetime, including in the *Wall Street Journal*, *Newsweek*, *New York Times* and *The Freeman*. He served for many years as a trustee of the Foundation for Economic Education (FEE) and was its founding vice president. His inspiration for this essay was the French economist Frédéric Bastiat. The most notable of Hazlitt's many books was the popular *Economics in One Lesson*, available for no charge at FEE.org.

Sandy Ikeda is a professor of economics at Purchase College, SUNY and the author of *The Dynamics of the Mixed Economy: Toward a Theory of Interventionism*. He is a regular contributor to *The Freeman*.

B. K. Marcus is managing editor of *The Freeman*, the magazine of the Foundation for Economic Education.

Wendy R. McElroy is a contributing editor of the Foundation for Economic Education's magazine, *The Freeman*, editor of ifeminists.com, and Research Fellow at The Independent Institute.

Edmund A. Opitz authored *Religion and Capitalism: Allies, Not Enemies* and other works. The Reverend Opitz served on the senior staff of the Foundation for Economic Education (FEE) for many years.

Paul L. Poirot was a long-time editor of *The Freeman*, the magazine of the Foundation for Economic Education.

Sheldon Richman was editor of *The Freeman*, the Foundation for Economic Education's magazine, for 15 years.

Ron Robinson is president of Young America's Foundation. *USA Today* notes that Robinson "has been involved in conservative campus issues for three decades." *Time* magazine wrote that Young America's "[F]oundation—run by former Reagan Administration advisor, Ron Robinson—is now the nation's largest advocacy group devoted to student politics." *Time* referred to Robinson as one of the "seasoned generals of the right" who is leading the "diverse and well funded" generation of conservatives who are "winning battles on campus." He is also the co-author with Nicole Hoplin of *Founding Fathers: The Unsung Heroes of the Conservative Movement*.

Hans F. Sennholz was chairman of the department of economics at Grove City College in Pennsylvania from 1956 to 1992. A noted economist and teacher of the Austrian school, he earned his Ph.D. under the tutelage of Ludwig von Mises. He was president of the Foundation for Economic Education from 1992 to 1997.

Tyler Watts is an Assistant Professor of Economics at East Texas Baptist University. His research has appeared in the *Independent Review*, the *Review of Austrian Economics*, and the *Journal of Private Enterprise*.

Walter Williams is a prominent commentator and has served on the faculty of George Mason University in Fairfax, Virginia as John M. Olin Distinguished Professor of Economics since 1980. He is the author of more than 150 scholarly journal articles.

SUGGESTED READING LIST

THOSE WHO HAVE ENJOYED THE CONTENT IN THIS BOOK SHOULD EXPLORE THE following titles to delve further into the topics covered herein. Additionally, you can discover other interesting content at the websites of the Foundation for Economic Education and Young America's Foundation found respectively at www.FEE.org and www.yaf.org.

Titles in the Suggested Reading List followed by an asterisk are available for no charge at www.FEE.org.

PHILOSOPHY & POLITICAL THEORY

A Conflict of Visions by Thomas Sowell
Anarchy, State, and Utopia by Robert Nozick
The Discovery of Freedom by Rose Wilder Lane
Funding Fathers by Nicole Hoplin and Ron Robinson
In Defense of Freedom by Frank S. Meyer
The Law by Frédéric Bastiat*

Liberal Fascism by Jonah Goldberg
The Libertarian Mind by David Boaz
On Liberty by John Stuart Mill
The Rational Optimist by Matt Ridley
Restoring the Lost Constitution by Randy Barnett
Upstream: The Ascendance of American Conservatism by Al Regnery

CULTURE

Are We Good Enough for Liberty? by Lawrence W. Reed*
Bourgeois Dignity by Deirdre N. McCloskey
God and Man at Yale by William F. Buckley
The Invisible Hand in Popular Culture by Paul Cantor
Mere Christianity by C.S. Lewis
The Rise and Fall of Society by Frank Chodorov
The Theme is Freedom by M. Stanton Evans
The Theory of Moral Sentiments by Adam Smith
The Virtue of Prosperity by Dinesh D'Souza

ECONOMICS

Anything That's Peaceful by Leonard E. Read*
Basic Economics by Thomas Sowell
Capitalism and Freedom by Milton Friedman
Economics In One Lesson by Henry Hazlitt*
The Government Against the Economy by George Reisman
I, Pencil by Leonard E. Read*
Individualism and Economic Order by F.A. Hayek
Liberalism by Ludwig von Mises
Liberty vs. the Tyranny of Socialism: Controversial Essays by Walter
    Williams
The Price of Everything by Russell Roberts
The Use of Knowledge in Society by F.A. Hayek*

HISTORY (U.S.)

Conceived in Liberty by Murray Rothbard

Constitution of the United States

Crisis and Leviathan by Robert Higgs

Declaration of Independence

The Federalist Papers by Alexander Hamilton

Great Myths of the Great Depression by Lawrence W. Reed*

New Deal or Raw Deal by Burt Folsom

HISTORY (WORLD)

A Republic—If We Can Keep It by Lawrence W. Reed and Burton W. Folsom*

Greatness: Reagan, Churchill and the Making of Extraordinary Leaders by Steven Hayward

Heaven on Earth: The Rise and Fall of Socialism by Joshua Muravchik

The History of Liberty by Lord Acton

The President, The Pope, and The Prime Minister by John O'Sullivan

Reflections on the Revolution in France by Edmund Burke

The Triumph of Liberty by Jim Powell

We also recommend Regnery Publishing's Politically Incorrect Guide® book series, which offers readers further insight into a number of topics including the Founding Fathers, the environment, the Constitution, the Bible, the Civil War and more.

INDEX

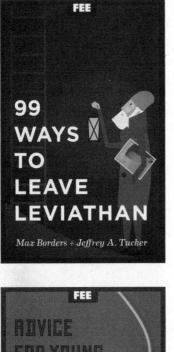

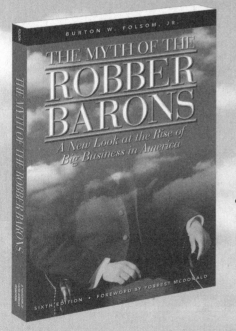